The law of trusts
and their uses
in Nigeria

Malthouse Law Books

Abdulrazaq, M. T., *Revenue Law in Nigeria*
Adah C. E., *The Nigerian Law of Evidence*
Bambale, Y. Y., *Crimes and Punishments under Islamic Law*
Igweike, K., *Nigerian Commercial Law: Agency*
Igweike, K., *Nigerian Commercial Law: Hire Purchase*
Igweike, K., *Nigerian Commercial Law: Contract*
Fogam, P., *Law of Contract*
Omorogbe, Yinka, *Oil and Gas Law in Nigeria*
Sagay, I., *Nigerian Family Law: Principles, Cases, Statutes and Commentaries*
Sagay, I., *Law of Succession and Inheritance*
Shoyele O., *Principles and Practice of Administrative Law in Nigeria*
Udombana, N., *Human Rights Issues in Africa*
Utuama, A. A., *Nigerian Planning Law*
Utuama, A. A., *Nigerian Law of Real Property*
Utuama, A. A., *The Law of Trusts and their Uses in Nigeria*
Uvieghara E. E., *Labour Law in Nigeria*
Uvieghara E. E., *Sale of Goods*
Yakubu J. A., *Limits to the Application of Foreign Laws*
Yakubu J. A., *Harmonisation of Laws in Africa*
Yakubu J. A., *International Contracts: Evolution and Theory*
Yakubu J. A., *Law of contract in Nigeria*
Yakubu J. A., *Press Law in Nigeria*
Yakubu J. A., *Administration of Justice in Nigeria*
Yakubu J. A. and Oyewo A. T., *Criminal Law and Procedure in Nigeria*

The law of trusts
and their uses
in Nigeria

edited by

Professor A. A. Utuama
Mr G. M. Ibru

malthouse Ɲ

Malthouse Press Limited

Lagos, Benin, Ibadan, Jos, Oxford, Zaria

Malthouse Press Limited
11B Goriola Street, Off Adeola Odeku
Victoria Island, Lagos
E-mail: malthouse_press@yahoo.com
Tel: 01-773 53 44, 01-613 957, 0802 364 2402

Lagos Benin Ibadan Jos Oxford Port-Harcourt Zaria

© A. A. Utuama and G. M. Ibru 2004
First published 2004
ISBN 978 023 174 9
ISBN-13: 978-978-023-174-3

Distributors:
African Books Collective Ltd
Unit 13, Kings Meadow
Ferry Hinksey Road
Oxford, OX2 0DP, UK
Tel: +44 - (0) 1865 -726686
Fax: +44 - (0) 1865 -793298
Email: abc@africanbookscollective.com
Website: http://www.africanbookscollective.com

Preface

This book is derived from papers presented at a seminar on uses of trust in the administration of property. The seminar was the second of a series of seminars on wills, trusts and settlements inaugurated by G. M. Ibru & Co to provide legal education on the options available for the administration of property *inter vivos* or posthumously with the object to secure the integrity of donor's intention and expectations of beneficiaries. The series started on the 5th February 1998 with the seminar on wills at which four papers were presented by experts on the subject. That seminar gave birth to the first book in the Law Seminar Series entitled *Law of Wills in Nigeria* published by Shaneson C. I. Ltd., 2001. The need for the publication of this book, like the first work, is underscored by the numerous issues of diverse interests generated by the discussion at the seminar and the high intellectual quality of the papers.

Although the papers were written by legal practitioners, this book is by no means an exclusive work for the legal practitioners law teachers and students only. It is an invaluable digest of the law on trusts for the prospective settlors, philanthropists, accountants, estate valuers and the successful individual. The book contains a discussion of the concept and overview of trust, appointment, role and standard of care of the trustees, uses of trusts in our society.

The book, as the reader will discover, is a lucid inquiry into the sociological nature, function, adequacy or otherwise of trusts as a means of administration of property in Nigeria.

Among those who deserve immense gratitude for their contributions in various forms is Mr Goodie Ibru for his vision and commitment in conceiving and actualising the idea of the series of seminars and the publication of their intellectual products. The late I. I. Akapo, who as a partner in G. M. Ibru & Co was the chairman of the organizing committee of the seminar series and who had worked tirelessly to see to the successful take-off of the series, Mr Eddie Chukwura, the managing partner of G. M. Ibru & Co. who put at the disposal of the organising committee the necessary resources to organise the seminar and to publish this work. We cannot forget the legal practitioners and administrative staff of G. M. Ibru & Co for their dedication and deprivation in this effort. We give special thanks to Guy Saris Ltd, Ikeja Hotel Ltd and Sheraton Lagos Hotel & Towers for their contributions and support.

We must place on record the assistance of NIDB Trustees Ltd and Avis-Oyolu & Associates, a firm of consultant for their interests and collaborating with G. M. Ibru & Co in organising the seminar.

Finally, we give special thanks to our resource persons, as well as our participants for their contributions, which made the seminar and this book possible.

Professor A. A. Utuama
Mr G. M. Ibru

Table of contents

Table of cases

Table of statutes

Chapter 1

An overview of the concept of trust

– Professor M. I. Jegede

After my initial assessment of what may be required of me in the consideration of the topic, my first reaction was to approach it by simply analysing, in its practical term, the application of the law of trust to the management of property. I, however, consider that this approach may be too narrow for two reasons. First, the general theme of the seminar is "The management of property - The trust Option", which to my mind is flexible and encompassing, and requires reasonable consideration of what is trust *simpliciter* on the one hand and the practical application of the law of trust in the management of property on the other. Since my topic is only a sub-theme, it is not unlikely in my view that the practical application of the law of trust in relation to management of property may be the subject-matter of another sub-theme of the seminar. This is reinforced by the fact that my sub-theme would appear narrow and theoretical. Second, limiting my paper to the practical application of the law of trust to management of property may rightly or wrongly be predicated on the assumption that the audience is composed of mainly people who are learned in law and, therefore, familiar with equity jurisprudence with particular reference to the origin and development of the equitable institution of trust. To avoid a dry and narrow approach, and at the same time avoid unnecessary and sometime boring repetition, I have decided on a mixed approach which is a consideration of the topic in the context of the origin and development of the institution of trust and its modern relevance in the management of property.

The received English law of trust

Simply put, the modern rules of equity owe their origin and development to the English Court of Chancery and were formally received into the Nigerian legal system through various statutory enactments.[1] If I may emphasize, the concept of trust is an institution of equity received into the Nigerian legal system and, like all equitable institutions and remedies, any claim arising from trust must be shown to have an ancestry founded in history and in the practice and precedents of the courts administering equity jurisdiction.[2] In the circumstance, a brief analysis of the origin and development of rules of trust law by the English Chancery is *sine qua non;* otherwise the language of English law of trust, which is commonly used in the administration of Nigerian property law, may not be properly appreciated.

The origin of the English Law of Trust bristles with difficulties. In the language of a modern equity scholar, the ultimate origin of the concept of use or trust is still one of the controversial topics of jurisprudence.[3]

The enforcement of trust by the Chancery is perhaps the most outstanding interference with the common law jurisdiction exercised because of the chancery's exercise of its exclusive jurisdiction. Indeed the jurisdiction exercised by the chancery in the enforcement of trust is likened to a legislative power, in the sense that the chancery not only deprived the legal owner of property of all the benefits in the property, but also created a distinct title on the same piece of property for the beneficiary. This title was unknown to any statute and at the same time was repudiated in no uncertain terms by the common law of the land.[4]

Such a feat of ingenuity demonstrated by the chancery cannot but be of interest to both early and contemporary equity scholars. Broadly, there are two different schools of thought with respect to the origin of trust, and each of these schools has attracted eminent disciples.

For example, Blackstone, in his *Commentaries on English Law*, claims that trusts are very similar in nature to the Roman *Fidei Commissum*. The *Fidei Commissum* was a disposal of inheritance to one with the understanding and confidence that the transferee would dispose of the property and or its profits at the will of another.

This method of disposing property was usually created by will, but the enforcement of the rights in the property so created inescapably led to a split in the title to property rights. The legal right, *jus fiduciarium*, was vested in the transferee, and was remedied and protected by the ordinary course of law, and a right in trust, *jus legitimum* was remedied and protected on the ground of conscience by the *praector*. The remedies provided by the praector were not

[1] See S.45 Interpretation Act Cap 89, 1958 Laws of Nigeria; S.14, High Court Law of Eastern Nigeria. Cap 61, Laws of Eastern Nigeria 1963; S.28 High Court Law of Northern Nigeria, Cap 49 Laws of Northern Nigeria 1963; S.4 Laws of England (Application) Law (W.N) Cap 60 Laws of Western Nigeria 1959.
[2] *Re Diplock* (1948) Ch. 465.
[3] Keeton, *The Law of Trusts* (6ᵗʰ Ed) 1963 P. 14 Spence, Court of Chancery (1846) Vol 1, p. 435
[4] See Spence, Court of Chancery (1846) vol. 1 p.435

predicated on any binding rules of law. From this standpoint, a very close connection was drawn between this remedy and the remedy provided by the chancery in the enforcement of uses of trust. It was, therefore, concluded that this notion was transplanted into England from the civil law by means of foreign ecclesiastics who introduced it to evade the statutes of mortmain by obtaining grants of lands, not to religious houses directly, but to the use of religious houses which the clerical chancellors of those times held to be *fidei commissa* and binding in conscience and, therefore, assumed the jurisdiction which Augustus had vested in his praector of compelling the execution of such in the court of chancery.[5] Indeed Spence believes that we must look to the Roman jurisprudence for the origin of trust, although what was to be found there was greatly extended and improved upon by the clerical chancellors and their successors.[6] It is contended that at the very end of the Roman republic, there was a law prohibiting succession to property by a female as heir, even if this female was the only child. Naturally, the society could not tolerate the absoluteness of such an unjust law for long. A device was, therefore, introduced whereby in such circumstance property would be conveyed by will to a qualified citizen, with a request that the devisee would restore the property to some person who otherwise, could not have taken the benefit under the Republican law. Initially, the fulfilment of this request depended on the absolute honesty and willingness of the devisee. And since what had transpired was an ingenious attempt to evade the law of the land, the law would not aid the enforcement of the request. But as the practice was becoming popular, and in order to prevent the rising breaches of such confidence, Augustus decreed its performance, later known in Roman legal history as the *fidei commissia*. Thus, the recognition of a concept of property ownership very similar to the modern law of trust was dictated by social pressure and the need to avoid a state of affairs whereby people in whom solemn confidence had been reposed would fraudulently breach this confidence.

Like the common law attitude to the enforcement of use, the Roman law regarded the devisee as the legal owner of the property. However, the rights of the beneficiary were constantly enforced by *Praectorian Actions* at a time when these actions were not tenable in the ordinary course of law. The original praectory nature of the *fidei commissa* later became imperative, in that the testator could use imperative words in his devise, which must be carried out to the letter by the appointed heir. When there was uncertainty about the words used by the testator, his intention as construed from the words became the controlling factor.[7] It is therefore, not impossible that similar principles being

---

[5] Blackstone's Comm.. (Lewis Ed)Bk. 2. 327-29
[6] Spence; Court of Chancery (1846) Vol. 1 P.435-36
[7] Spence, Ibid.

applied by the English courts in the construction of praectory trust[8] have originated from Roman idea.

Story[9] is not as assertive as either Blackstone or Spence in tracing the origin of uses to Roman jurisprudence. Because of their similarity to the Roman *fidei commissa* he believes that trusts, which had been within the exclusive jurisdiction of the courts of equity, were derived from the Roman law. He vindicates his view by saying that any country, which professed to possess an enlightened system of jurisprudence, must necessarily provide for the enforcement of the nature of duty imposed on the trustee. He gives a brief analysis of trust in the Roman law and as at last protected by Augustus, who yielded to popular practice by his appointment of a *praector* to protect the rights of beneficiaries under such trusts. He quotes Blackstone in support of the view that the origin and nature of trust in civil law illustrate, in a very striking manner, the origin and nature of trust in the English system.

On the other hand, the second school of thought believes that the origin of trust has no connection with Roman law. Maitland, with his veneration for the ability of English lawyers, in their development of the law of trust, denies that the origin of the English law of trust is traceable to the Roman *Fidei Commissum*. He said:

> Some have thought that this new jurisprudence of uses was borrowed from the Roman law, that the English use or trust is historically connected with the Roman *Fidei Commissum*. I do not myself believe in the connection. One reason for this disbelief I will at once state because it leads on to an important point. From the first, the chancellors seem to have treated the right of the *cestui que use* as very analogous to an estate in land. They brought to bear upon it the rules of the English land law as regards such matters as descent and the like.[10]

Maitland seems not to have seen anything Roman in the origin of uses. They are, for him, a natural outcome of ancient English elements, having their foundation in the common law rules of agency. These rules were later adopted in conveying land to the borough community to the use of the Franciscan Friars who, because of their oath of poverty, could not own any property.[11]

Holmes takes a view similar to Maitland. He traces the origin of the uses to *Salman* of the early German law. Like a trustee to whom land was conveyed that he might deal with it according to his grantor's directions, *Salman* held to the use of the grantor, in grantor's lifetime, and later to be disposed of after the grantor's death, according to grantor's directions. The essence of the relation

---

[8] *Knight v Knight* (1840) 49.ER.58; *Brown v Higgs* (1801-3) 32 E.R. 473
[9] *Equity Jurisprudence* (14th Ed) Vol.ll pp. 649-50 (1918).
[10] Maitland *Equity* (Brunyate Ed. 1949) p.32
[11] Maitland; *Collected Papers* Vol. 11 l pp.321-404

thus created from this transaction was the *fiducia* or trust reposed in the *fidelis manus* who sometimes confirmed his obligation by an oath or covenant:

> This likeness between the *Salman* and the *feofees* to use would be enough, without more, to satisfy me that the latter was the former transplanted.[12]

The *Salman* was an executor, and in the early years of use there was little or no distinction between executor and *feofee* to uses. He concludes, because of the close connection between Anglo-Norman law and Frankish tradition that uses must have originated from *Salman*:

> The foundation of the claim is the *fides,* the trust reposed and the obligation of good faith, and that circumstance remains as a mark at once of the Teutonic source of the right and the ecclesiastical origin of the jurisdiction.[13]

Holdsworth's view is similar; the mere fact that the use is analogous to *fidei commissum* does not mean it originated from it. He contends that a trust of property to someone by another for a purpose is present in any society with a recognized legal system, however rudimentary.

Personal actions like detinue, which protected ownership and possession at common law, strengthen the view that the idea of uses originated from common law.[14]

It is not an easy task to attempt to discredit any of these theories about the historical origin of uses. First, all the theories point to what may be the origin of uses; and second, there is the difficulty of checking the various historical connections with the suggested origins.

However, it is true that the Roman *fidei commisum* is very much analogous to the feofee to uses. It is also true that English law generally borrowed much from the Roman system, and that the ecclesiastics who first enforced uses in the chancery were very learned in Roman law. Therefore, it is quite possible that these chancery clerics might have been influenced by the *fidei commisum* of Rome in their enforcement of the uses in England. But as Holdsworth points out, analogy alone is not a sufficient criterion to infer a common origin. This, of course, applies to Holmes' assimilation of the use to the Teutonic *Salman,* a view to which Holdsworth himself accedes. Keeton is probably right when he observes that it would be as false to derive the modern office personal representative from trusteeship as it is unnecessary to derive the office of trustee from that of the primitive executor.[15] Keeton's[16] view that the basic conception

---

[12] Holmes, *Early English Equity*; Uses. IL.Q.Rev (1885) 162 At P. 164
[13] Ibid., at 170
[14] Holdworth; *History of English Law* (1924) Vol.IV 410-417
[15] Keeton, *The Law of Trusts* (8th Edn), p.15
[16] *Op. cit.*

of a use is fundamental, and that it appears in several systems of law, though the working out of its legal incidents eventually exhibits considerable differences, seems to be more acceptable than theories founded mainly on analogies and dubious historical connections.

Whatever may be the true origin of uses, it is to the early chancellors that the modern Anglo-American law of trust owes its development. Considering the expensive way in which trust is being used in the modern period, it becomes difficult to resist the suggestion that the greatest contribution to the substantive law, which has ever been set down to the credit of the chancery, is the enforcement of uses.[17] They are, indeed, a distinctive improvement invented and nurtured in a relatively high state of civilization which common law was too archaic to deal with. Through the recognition and enforcement of the beneficiary's interest, a split in title was created. Thus in the Anglo-American law of trust, there are the legal and the equitable rights existing in the same property at the same time and the duty of the trustee is made obligatory by law. These are what that make the Anglo-American law of trust unique.[18]

As Scott rightly observed, trust is unique because it affords the most flexible device for making dispositions of property. Through the trust it is possible to separate the benefit of ownership from the burdens of ownership,[19] thus creating a double ownership in the same property. The number of ways through which trust could be adapted, perhaps, justifies Maitland's eulogy and veneration of the doctrine. In fact, a doctrine of jurisprudence which now applies to a considerable part of the national wealth of common law jurisdiction could be rightly regarded as the greatest and most distinctive achievement performed by Englishmen in the field of jurisprudence.[20] Through the trust, technical and complex rules of conveyance which have long plagued conveyance at law have been avoided.

Because of its flexible adaptation, it could be used to translate progressive ideas into reality and for this reason; trust has become an instrument of legal change. Trust has not been free from certain abuses, but what is striking is that, even in its very early development, the chancery did not hesitate in devising means to check these abuses. To this end, various equitable maxims had been developed. For example, "he who wants equity must do equity" and "he who wants equity must come with clean hands." These are to prevent the rules of equity, which are based on conscience and sound policy, from being used as a vehicle for fraud.[21]

The importance of the modern law of trust seems to have been neatly summed up in the observation that:

---

[17] Ames, *The Origin of Uses and Trusts* 21 Harv. L. Rev 261 At 265 (1907).
[18] Holmes, *Early English Equity Uses* I L. Qren (1885) 162
[19] *Scott On Trusts*, Vol. 1 (2nd Ed 1956), p. 4
[20] *Maitland Equity* (Brunyate Ed) 1936 p.20
[21] *Scott On Trusts* (2nd Ed) Vol. 1 P.20

The old philosophy of uses evolved by the chancellors of the fifteenth century, and rendered more subtle and intricate by the courts of law in the sixteenth century, gave way to a new philosophy of trust based upon clearer conceptions of public policy and of the nature and purposes of the law.[22]

Definition of a trust

Like many other definitions of legal terms, no definition of a trust appears to have been accepted as both comprehensive and exact.[23] Generally, definitions are always wrought with difficulties and are often said in the law to be perilous and unsatisfactory.

However, Professor Keeton seems to give a fairly satisfactory definition which includes all the significant features of a trust, when he says, "all that can be said of a trust therefore, is that it is the relationship which arises wherever a person called the trustee is compelled in equity to hold property, whether real or personal, and whether by legal or equitable title, for the benefit of some persons (of whom he may be one and who are termed *cestui que trust)* or for some object permitted by law, in such a way that the real benefit of the property accrues, not to the trustee, but to the beneficiaries or other objects of the trust."[24]

It is clear that trust is a device for making disposition of property interest, and the system of ownership implicit in this device may be peculiar to English jurisprudence. Trust in English law has created a double system of ownership in one property that is unknown to many other legal systems including the Nigerian Customary Law concept of trusteeship.[25] The trustee, under English law, holds the nominal but at the same time dominant ownership recognized at law, but in equity, the beneficial interest is vested in the beneficiary. The ownership of the trustee creates a special relationship (fiduciary in character) with respect to trust property. This relationship imposes on the trustee certain equitable duties and obligations, enforceable in equity against the trustee by any person (beneficiary under the trust) who has beneficial interest in the trust property. Along with the trustee's duties and obligations, there are, vested in him, certain powers and discretions the purpose of which is efficient control and management of the trust property. The trustee is absolutely responsible for the exercise of his powers (with some statutory restrictions) though in equity he must exercise these powers in accordance with the instrument creating the trust and for the benefit of the beneficiaries. Here lies the reason for the statement that "through the trust, it

---

[22] Ibid at 24
[23] *Underhills Law of Trusts and Trustee* (11th Ed) (1959) P.3
[24] *The Law of Trusts* (8th Ed) p..3
[25] See M.I. Jegede, "The position of the head of family in relation to family property" (1966), *Nigerian Bar Journal*, P.21

is possible to separate the benefits of ownership from the burdens of ownership."[26]

The foregoing highlights the striking features of the English law of trust, the main principles of which have been formally received into the Nigerian legal system. Although, much has been said and written about the peculiarities and distinctiveness, trust, as an institution is not peculiar to English jurisprudence. However, it is conceded that the split of title into two with respect to the same property corresponding to the distinction between common law and equity which splits into two parts the English legal system, makes the English trust concept alien to Nigerian Customary law concept of trusteeship and those of other countries having Roman law as the foundation of their legal system.

Creation of trust

In real terms, the institution of trust has become a veritable means in the sphere of property management, particularly in countries having common law as the cornerstone of their legal system. It is, therefore, not out of tune that trust is gradually becoming acceptable in the realm of administration and management of property in Nigeria.

Though the institution of trust is apparently simple, attractive and flexible, there are certain basic requirements that must be satisfied before it can be said in legal terms that a trust has been perfectly constituted. Before my brief analysis of these requirements, I would like to emphasize that trust in general involves a kind of triangular connection points. First, there is the point of the settlor, i.e. the creator of the trust; second, there is the trustee, i.e. the person who is to carry the burden of managing the trust property; the third, the beneficiary who, as the name implies, enjoys the benefits of the trust.

The law relating to the constitution of a trust would seem to have been settled notwithstanding some ad-hoc statutory interventions, which have not derogated from the laid down principles.

As far back as 1862, the English Court of Appeal in Chancery laid down the following, which have since been consistently followed. Turner L.J. in *Milroy* v *Lord*[27] said:

> I take the law of this court to be well settled, that in order to render a voluntary settlement valid and effectual the settlor must have done everything which according to the nature of the property comprised in the settlement was necessary to be done in order to transfer the property and render the settlement binding upon him. He may, of course, do this by actually

---

[26] *Scott On Trusts*, Vol .I (2nd Ed) 1956 p.4
[27] (1862) 4 De G.F. & J. 264 at 274-75.

transferring the property to the persons for whom he intends to provide, and the provision will be effectual, and it will be equally effectual if he transfers the property to a trustee for the purpose of settlement, or declares that he himself holds it in trust for those purpose; and if the property be personal, the trust may as I apprehend, be declared either in writing or by parol. But in order to render the settlement binding, one or other of these modes must be resorted to, for there is no equity in this court to perfect an imperfect gift. The cases go further to the extent that if the settlement is intended to be effectuated by one of the modes to which I have referred the court will not give effect to it by applying another of those modes. If it is intended to take effect by transfer, the court will not hold the intended transfer to operate as a declaration of trust, for then every imperfect instrument would be made effectual by being converted into a perfect trust.

The message here to any intending settlor is that the transfer of the trust property to the trustees must be appropriate and in accord with the rules and modes applicable to the property concerned, i.e. the subject matter of the trust. For example, where the subject matter of the intended trust is land, it has to be transferred in accordance with the prevailing mode of transferring land. The transfer of land must not only be by deed, the consent of the governor must first be sought and obtained, otherwise such transfer may be null and void. Although this notorious and controversial provision in the Land Use Decree is apparently intended to be employed in the control and effective utilization of land, it has regrettably been turned to an instrument for raking prohibitive fees from purchasers of landed property to the extent that it has now become an unwelcome clog in the process of land transactions. Consequently, it has unwittingly restricted alienation of land, whereas for purposes of commerce, land should be seen as a commercial commodity, which ought to be easily alienable in terms of cost and procedure.

The full effect of the provision, with regard to the creation of trust of land *inter vivos* for purposes of management, is to discourage a settlor who will be concerned not only with the notorious delay in the process of obtaining consent but also with the prohibitive cost, because it is not in doubt that there cannot be an effective transfer, if the required consent is not sought and obtained, and, to constitute a trust the subject matter of the trust must be properly and effectively transferred to the trustee.

Where the subject matter of the trust is personal property, the position would appear to be relatively simpler. In case of shares, they must be transferred by the appropriate procedure, which is usually provided by the memorandum and articles of association of the company concerned. This is the case in respect of private companies. However, shares in public companies may involve a number of complications, certainly not as easy as transfer of shares in private companies because of a number of statutory regulatory authorities involved in dealings affecting shares in public companies.

In other personal properties, effective transfer largely depends on the nature of the property and relevant statutory provisions. For example transfer of chose in action, such as copyright and designs are governed by the appropriate statutory provisions.

What is of utmost importance is that the subject matter of the intended Trust must be effectively transferred to the Trustee before it can be said that the trust is completely constituted. Once this is done, the trustee is regarded as the legal owner of the property governed only by the directives in the Trust instrument and the well-established equitable principles relevant to the duties and responsibilities of a Trustee in relation to his trust. At this juncture, it has to be emphasized that once the property has been vested in the Trustee, the settlor, i.e. the creator of the trust is no longer in a position to reclaim the property, indeed the only duty of the trustee from that point in time is towards the beneficiary of the trust.

In constituting a trust, the settlor would be concerned with the capability of the trustee. This is of great importance in cases where trustees will be saddled with the duty of managing trust property for the benefit of beneficiaries or the purposes for which the trust was created. Thus the choice of a trustee ought to be determined by the qualification of the trustee in relation to the property, which is the subject matter of the trust. In other words, if efficient management of property (which, as aforesaid, is the subject matter of the trust) is the driving force behind the creation of the trust, it is of utmost importance for the settlor to ensure that he appoints a fit and proper person, in terms of qualifications and experience, as trustee of the trust. To this end the law has provided a number of options for the settlor. Depending on the nature and purpose of the trust, the settlor may appoint any person who in law is able to hold property, as trustee. Thus, a minor may not be appointed a trustee of land because being a minor he is not legally capable of holding a legal estate in land. Trustees, statutorily designated as judicial trustees, may be appointed under the Judicial Trustees Act. Such appointment may be made in different circumstances. A person intending to create a trust may apply to the court to appoint a person as judicial trustee. In some other circumstances, the court may on the application of a beneficiary appoint a judicial trustee of a trust, particularly where the administration of the trust by the ordinary trustees had broken down. Whenever a judicial trustee is appointed, such trustee acts in close concert with the court.

The public trustee may also be appointed under the Public Trustee Act. The public trustee is a corporation sole whose liabilities for breach of trust is covered by the state.

He may be appointed as ordinary trustee, acting solely or jointly with others. He may also act as a Custodian Trustee. The Public Trustee is entitled to charge fees for his services to the trust. The appointment of public trustee as trustee for the purposes of managing property is not advisable because of the proven incompetence of the Department of Public Trustee in the management of trust property.

Trust corporations may also be appointed as trustees. These are mainly public corporations, which are permitted by their Memorandum and Articles of Association to act as trustees. Public companies such as banks and insurance companies usually have separate departments for the business of executors and trusteeship within their establishments. These are professional trustees with unrivalled facilities and they are equally permanent and dependable. Depending on the nature and the size of the trust, solicitors and accountants may be appointed as trustees; their professional calling in terms of management of trust property readily recommend them as fit and proper persons to be appointed trustees. Whatever may be the case, in the appointment of trustees for the management of property, no effort should be spared to ensure that the right person or persons are appointed.

It cannot be overemphasised that the office of a trustee in relation to his trust is an onerous one. It is rightly stated that in the performance of his office, a trustee must act exclusively in the interest of the trust. He is supposed to act disinterestedly. In other words, he should stand to gain nothing from his work except where there is a special and express provision in the trust instrument authorising his remuneration. He is required to observe the highest standards of integrity and a reasonable standard of business efficiency in the management of the affairs of the trust and he would be held personally liable if he falls below the required standard in his duties to the trust.[28]

In view of the disinterested requirement of the office and the inherent burden in the performance of the incidental duties, the office of trustee is not an attractive one. However, professional trustees see it as business and would readily accept the office provided there is an express provision in the trust instrument authorising their remuneration. Where a non-professional trustee is appointed, he is permitted to employ professionals such as accountants, solicitors, management consultants and the like, provided administration of the trust demands such appointments.

Whichever way one looks at it, the institution of the trust has provided a solid platform through which anyone who may so desire can arrange for the efficient management of his property either by creating a trust *inter vivos* or by *will*. There are in the country today, a large number of people who have acquired stupendous wealth through various means. Such wealth could still be preserved for the family and ultimately for the benefit of the society at large through the institution of trust *inter vivos*. This is accomplished by transferring assets to the trustee with specific directives in the trust instrument as to who the beneficiaries are and what each of them is entitled to. In effect, distribution of family fortune

---

[28] See generally, *Hanbury and Maudsley; Modern Equity* (12th Ed) By J.E. Martin (1985), p. 471-73.

by the creation of trust *inter vivos* may protect such fortune from acrimonious and wasteful litigation which now characterise disposition of property by will or in the cases of intestacy. It needs to be mentioned too that many potentially liable enterprises usually collapse at the death of the founders. This may arise because of acrimony among other founding members of the deceased's establishment or because of incompetence on the part of family members in the management of the deceased's business interest. It is more likely that making such business interest the subject matter of a trust would preserve it not only for the immediate members of the family but also that of generations yet unborn, after all, it is well know that many of the great multi-national corporations currently operating in our country originated from family enterprises.

Perhaps another very important factor in the creation of trusts *inter vivos* is the incidence of taxation. The more a person acquires in capital and property terms, the higher will be the rates of taxation. To avoid payment of high rate of taxation, a wealthy person can share out his wealth by creating trust *inter vivos*. The tax liability is thereby drastically reduced in the setlor's lifetime and when he dies, estate duty will only be payable on what he owned at the time his death.

Subject to certain restrictions and some technical tax rules, which are not relevant for discussion in this chapter, such trust *inter vivos*, are perfectly legitimate modes of tax avoidance; after all, Lord Tomlin in *I.R.C.* v *Duke of Westminister* said "every man is entitled if he can to order his affairs so that the tax attaching under the appropriate Acts is less than it otherwise would be."[29]

Standard of conduct-trustee

As stated earlier, the duties of trustees are as contained in the trust instruments and other well-established equitable principles and relevant statutory provisions. In carrying out these duties, the trustee is required to maintain a standard of conduct depending on whether he is an unpaid trustee, paid trustee or professional trustee. In the case of an unpaid trustee, in the discharge of his duties, he is expected to take the precaution, which an ordinary prudent man of business would take in managing similar affairs of his own.[30] This is a simple objective test. But in the case of paid trustees who are usually professionals, such as solicitors and accountants, higher standards are imposed. They are expected to exercise higher standards of diligence and knowledge than unpaid trustees. Thus, a Bank that advertises itself in the public press as being capable of taking charge of administration is under a special duty in relation to the management of trust.[31]

---

[29] (1936) AC I at p.19
[30] See *Speight* v *Gaunt* (1883) 9 App. Cas 1.
[31] *Re Waterman's Will Trusts* (1952) 2 All ER 1054 At 1055

This position was recently emphasised by an English judge when he said,

> I am of the opinion that a higher duty of care is plainly due from someone like a trust corporation which carries on a specialized business of trust management. A trust corporation holds itself out in its advertising literature as being above ordinary mortals. With a specialist staff of trained trust officer and managers, The trust corporation holds itself out, and rightly, as capable of providing an expertise which it would be unrealistic to expect and unjust to demand from the ordinary prudent man or woman who accepts, probably unpaid and sometime reluctantly from a sense family duty, the burdens of a trusteeship...so I think that a professional corporate trustee is liable for breach of trust if loss is caused to the trust fund because it neglects to exercise the special care and skill which it professes to have.[32]

Whichever category a trustee finds himself in, he is liable for a breach of trust resulting from his failure to meet the standard required of him. The remedies provided for breach of trust include personal action against the trustee, tracing the trust property, and removal of the offending trustee. In cases where the breach of trust amounts to a crime, the trustee may be subject to criminal prosecution.

---

[32] Brightman J. in *Barlett* v *Barclays Bank Trust Co. Ltd* (No. 1)(1980 Ch 515 At 534).

Chapter 2

Appointment, powers, and duties of trustees

- Professor Gaius Ezejiofor (SAN)

Introduction

The trust concept is probably the most outstanding contribution of English
Jurisprudence. There are several definitions of the concept, and it seems to me
that the least complicated of them all is the one rendered by Cheshire. According
to him

> A trust arises when property is vested in a person, called the trustee, who is
> bound to hold and administer that property on behalf of another person called
> the beneficiary, or *cestui que trust,* whether the obligation is created
> expressly, or by implication or by operation of law.[1]

The implication of this definition is that trusts can arise in several different
ways. Thus, there can be express, implied, resulting or constructive trusts. The
focus of this paper is on express trusts, which are those that are intentionally and
deliberately created by a person in an instrument such as a deed or a will.

The principles of equity, the English Trustee Act, 1893, and State Trustee
laws regulate the institution of the trust in this country. The Trustee Act is a
statute of general application, and applies in those states that have not enacted
laws to regulate the administration of trusts within their jurisdictions. In 1959,
the defunct Western Region of Nigeria enacted, among others, the Trustee law.[2]
This has been adopted by all the states that were created out of the region.[3]

---

[1] *Modern Law of Real Property*, 11th Ed. (1972), p. 350
[2] Cap. 125, Laws of Western Nigeria, 1959.
[3] See for example, Cap. 128, Laws of Oyo State, 1978; Cap. 126, Laws of Ondo State, 1978; Cap
130, Laws of Ogun State, 1978.

Again, in 1986, the old Anambra State enacted the Trust and Equity Law,[3a] which is in force in the new Anambra State and the states created out of it.

The Trustee Act and the various Trustee Laws contain almost identical provisions in respect of the subject of this paper. For reasons of convenience, I shall hereunder cite only the Trustee Act and the parent Trustee Law, i.e. that of the Western Region of Nigeria.

Trustees are perhaps the most important single elements that determine the operational efficacy, or lack of it, of a trust. This chapter, therefore, examines issues relating to their appointment, the determination of such appointment as well as their duties and powers.

Appointment of original trustees

Any person of full age and capacity can be appointed a trustee. Trust corporations, i.e. corporate bodies empowered by the court or statute to conduct the business of trusteeship can also be appointed. These include banks, other financial institutions and insurance companies. The Public Trustee can be appointed an ordinary trustee or a guardian trustee.[3b] The questions, which must be considered by a person who wants to set up a trust are:

- Who should he appoint?
- Should he appoint one or more persons?
- Should they be professionals or non-professionals?
- Should he appoint a trust corporation or such a corporation and natural persons?
- What would happen if the person appointed disclaims, dies, resigns, becomes incapable of acting, does not perform or does not get on with the beneficiaries?

Thus, one sees that it is the sole responsibility of a person who desires to set up a trust to ensure that he appoints as a trustee, an honest man of integrity who is in a position to devote his time to the business of the trust. It is also his duty to decide whether he appoints a trust corporation, a professional or non-professional.

A sole trustee or any number of trustees may be appointed, since there is no restriction on the number of persons to be appointed except that the Trustee Law prescribes that more than four persons cannot be appointed as trustees for sale of

---

[3a] Cap. 132, Laws of Anambra State, 1986. There may be other States Trustee Laws which I am not aware of, but such laws, if they exist, are not likely to have provisions which are different from those in the laws mentioned in this chapter.

[3b] Public Trustee Act and Law, s. 9

land.[4] However, the appointment of a sole trustee is not advisable because of the risk of fraud or maladministration involved in entrusting the management of trust estate to one individual. Besides, the Trustee Law[5] provides that a sole trustee who is not a trust corporation cannot give a valid receipt for the proceeds of sale under a trust for sale of land. Unless the creator of the trust has honest and committed relations or friends who, because of their love and respect for him, would see the administration of the trust as a duty owed him, he is better advised to appoint a trust corporation or a professional who would execute the trust at a fee. Once the original trustee or trustees are prudently appointed the law takes care of the rest of the questions raised above, as is shown below.

Original trustees are normally appointed by the settlor or testator in the trust instrument, i.e. a will or a deed. A principle of equity is that "equity never wants for a trustee". Consequently if all the trustees in a settlement disclaim, the settlor will hold the trust property as trustee. And if all the trustees die, the personal representatives of the last survivor hold the property as trustees. Where they all die in a common disaster, the youngest is presumed to have survived the others.[6]

Appointment of new or additional trustees

To ensure that the administration of a trust is not disrupted as a result of depletion in the number of trustees, the law[7] makes provision for the filling of a vacancy whenever it occurs. A vacancy occurs when a serving trustee dies. In general, a trust can be affected in the following circumstances:

(i) The dissolution of a trust corporation is tantamount to its death.
(ii) If a member remains outside Nigeria for an uninterrupted period of more than twelve months.
(iii) If a member desires to be discharged or refuses to act.
(iv) If a member is unfit to act, such as where he is insolvent.
(v) If a member is incapable of acting, such as where he is too old or sick.

The question is *who makes the appointment?* In a settlement *inter vivos* the settlor may prescribe that he will appoint a new or an additional trustee. In the absence of such a provision he cannot make the appointment. Alternatively, the trust instrument may nominate a person or persons who will appoint. But there may be no such nomination or the nominated person may be unable or unwilling to act. In that case the appointment is made in writing by the surviving or

---

[4] S. 22
[5] S. 6(2)
[6] Evidence Act, s. 43(b)
[7] See Trustee Act, s.10 and Trustee Law, s.24

continuing trustees. If all the trustees are dead, the appointment is made by the personal representatives of the last surviving or continuing trustee.

Under the Trustee Law,[8] additional trustees may be appointed even when there is no vacancy, provided that none of the existing and continuing trustees is a trust corporation and the appointment does not bring the number to more than four. Such appointment is made in the same manner as has been described above.

A trustee who is removed from office for any reason cannot be re-appointed as a new trustee.[9] For example, a trustee who is removed on account of ill-health cannot be subsequently re-appointed when he recovers. Therefore, beneficiaries should be slow to apply for the removal of such a person unless it is manifestingly obvious that he cannot recover from the ill-health.[9a] The High Court is empowered to appoint new or additional trustee or trustees when it is expedient to appoint them, and when it is inexpedient, difficult, or impracticable to do so without the assistance of the court. In particular, the court may make an order for the appointment of a new trustee to replace one convicted of felony or one who is bankrupt.[10] The power of the court is rather limited because it has no jurisdiction to effect an appointment if the persons who have the statutory power to appoint object to the appointment, even if a majority of the beneficiaries have applied to the court for the appointment.[11]

The provision, which authorizes continuing and surviving trustees or their personal representatives to appoint new or additional trustees, can create problems. A person appointed in pursuance of this provision owes no moral obligation to the donor to be administered in the areas of honesty and diligence. They should, therefore, ensure that the right persons are appointed. And the appointees, once they accept to serve, will feel morally obliged to satisfy the expectations of the beneficiaries.

Fortunately the provision under consideration applies only when there is no contrary provision in the trust instrument.[12] Drafters of trust instrument are urged to advise the donor to nominate in the instrument the person or persons who will appoint new or additional trustees. Such nominees are likely to make appointments, which the donor would have himself made, were he to do so. And in the case of settlement *inter vivos* the settlor should nominate himself as the person who will appoint additional or new trustee. He should also nominate the person or persons who will make the appointment when he is dead.

---

[8] S. 24(6)
[9] *Olowu* v *Renner* (1968) NMLR
[9a] *Supra*
[10] Trustee Act, s. 25; Trustee Law, s.28
[11] *Re Higginbottom* (1882) 3 Ch. 132
[12] Trustee Act, s. 10(5): This statement is merely declaratory, for any statutory provision in this matter is necessarily subject to the express provisions in the trust instrument.

Determination of trusteeship

Disclaimer

A person appointed trustee does not have to accept to serve. He can disclaim. In other words, he can reject the appointment. Rejection may be express or by executing a deed to that effect. Very often the executor of a will is also appointed trustee by the testator. If the executor takes out probate he is deemed to have accepted the trust. But if he renounces probate, that is a strong evidence of the rejection of the trust.[13] To reduce the possibility of disclaimer to the barest minimum, donors are advised to sound out proposed appointees before the actual appointment. In this way opportunity is given to them to express their opinion on their willingness or otherwise to serve. A person who does not give a positive response will not be appointed in the first place. In this way the incidence of disclaimer is reduced.

Retirement

A trustee retires or is discharged on the appointment of a new one to replace him. Sometimes a trustee is allowed to retire even though no new one is appointed provided that at least two trustees or a trust corporation remain to administer the trust, and that he executes a deed instrument stating that he desires to retire and obtains the consent by deed of all the co- trustees and any person having the power to appoint new trustees. He also retires if he gets the consent of all the beneficiaries to do so. Finally, a trustee may retire pursuant to a power to do so in the instrument.

When a trustee retires he must do all that is necessary to vest the trust in the continuing trustees alone.

Removal by the Court

As we have seen above, the court has the statutory power to appoint a new trustee. Often such an appointment implies the removal of an existing one. This apart, the court has an inherent jurisdiction to remove a trustee compulsorily whether or not a new one is appointed to replace him. It will do so if it is satisfied that the trustee's continuance in office would be prejudicial to the due performance of the trust, and to the interests of the beneficiaries or if the trustee has disregarded his duties.[14] An example is where there is a friction between the trustee and the beneficiaries. This may be a sufficient reason to remove the

---

[13] *Nylander* v *Thomas* (1968) 1 All NLR 80
[14] *Adeseye* v *Williams* (1964) 2 All NLR 37

trustee even when he has committed no breach of the trust. The paramount consideration in the exercise of the court's power is the interest of the beneficiaries.[15] According to the court:

> it is clear that while the court will not remove trustees merely because of strained relations between the trustees and the *cesti que* trust, it is a matter to be taken into consideration in determining whether the trustees should be removed or not.[16]

Duties of Trustees

The office of a trustee is a very responsible one and as such imposes a very heavy burden on the holder. He hardly has any rights in respect of his office. He gains nothing unless the appointing instrument provides for the trust. He is required to observe a very high standard of integrity and is subjected to tremendous personal liability if he fails to reach this standard. He must not compete with the business of the trust nor put himself in a position where his personal interest conflicts with that of the trust. Indeed, he may be forced to forgo opportunities, which would be available to him if he were not a trustee.

Duty of care

Perhaps the foremost duty of a trustee is to exercise his functions with utmost care -*exacta diligentia*. In particular, if he is paid for his services, the degree of diligence and proficiency expected of him is that of a specialist in trust administration.[17] If a trustee is unpaid, then the degree of care and diligence expected of him, is not as heavy as if he was paid.

Specific duties

A trustee is obliged to observe the terms of the trust. In other words, he must endeavour to carry through the intentions of the donor as contained in the trust instrument. And the court would not normally authorize a deviation from such terms.[18]

---

[15] This is the rule in *Letterstedt* v *Broers* (1884) 9 App. Cas. 371
[16] *Williams* v *Bankole* ID/43/66 (Unreported)
[17] *Re Waterman's Will Trust* (1952) 2 All ER 1054 at p. 1055
[18] *Brice* v *Stocks* (1805) 11 Ves Jr 319; *Speight* v *Gaunt* (1883) 9 App. Cas. 1

The trustees must take possession of the trust property. In other words, the trust property must be collected by the trustees. If such property is a chose in action, such as a debt, the trustees must sue and collect the same if payment is not forthcoming. If the debt becomes statute-barred or otherwise irrecoverable, the trustees would be held liable. If the trust property includes a lease with an option to purchase the reversion, it is the duty of the trustees to exercise the option. All the trustees must have joint of control the trust property. If one of two joint trustees is allowed by the others to control the property and he misappropriates the same, the dormant one is guilty of breach of trust. Therefore, trust money should be paid into a bank and all the trustees should be signatories to the account. Non-negotiable securities and title deeds may, however, be in the possession of one them. Trustees are obliged to invest the trust property productively. But such investment must be in accordance with the directions in the trust instrument or as prescribed by law. In this connection the Trustee Investment Act[19] stipulates that a trustee can invest in the following securities:

(a) Federal Government Securities
(b) State Government Securities
(c) Securities of companies or corporations incorporated directly by an Act or Law and specified in the schedule to the Act[20]
(d) Debentures and fully paid shares of any company incorporated and registered under the CAMA, not being a private company.[21]

The Act contains provisions, which are designed to ensure that investment is not made in just any registered company, but only in healthy and viable ones. Thus, the power conferred on the trustees by the Act shall not be exercised unless at the time it is proposed to exercise it.[22]

1) the nominal value of the fully paid-up shares issued by the company is not less than one million naira;[23]
2) The shares or debentures are quoted in the Lagos Stock Exchange;
3) Dividends have been paid on all the shares during each of the 3 years immediately preceding the current one and the value of such dividend paid in each of the years was not less than 5% of the nominal value of the share.

---

[19] Cap 449, LFN 1990
[20] The Schedule names the following: Nigerian Coal Corporation, NEPA, Nigerian Ports Authority and Nigerian Railway Corporation.
[21] Ibid. ss. 2 & 3
[22] S. 2(2)
[23] This figure may be adequate when the Act was enacted but certainly not so now because of the astronomical fall in the value of the naira.

However no investment shall be made in exercise of the power under the Act if that would cause:

1. The value of the fund sought to be invested to exceed 1/3 of the total value of the fund.
2. The value of the fund invested in the share and debentures of a particular company to exceed 1/10 of the total value of the fund of the worth of the company.
3. The value of the fund sought to be invested in the shares and debentures of a particular company to exceed 1/20 of the total value of the fund.[24]

It is one of the obligations of trustees to keep proper account of their dealings in the trust property and any of the beneficiaries is entitled to inspect the account. He must be given access to it. But this does not imply that the trustees are obliged to reveal to a beneficiary, the reason for their exercise of discretion, in a particular matter. Consequently, if an inspection of the account or any document by a beneficiary would reveal to him the reasons for the exercise of discretion, then the trustees are entitled to disallow it.

A trustee occupies a fiduciary position in relation to the trust. Equity does not generally allow anybody in such a position to make a profit unless he is expressly authorized to do so. Therefore, a trustee must not make a profit form his administration of the trusts. Were he to do so, he would most likely put himself in a position where his interest would conflict with his duty. Because of the fiduciary nature of their position, trustees are ordinarily not paid for their services. They are expected to act voluntarily and gratuitously. But it may be questioned, why would a person accept such an onerous and almost thankless job when he is not to be remunerated?

Some members of the donor's family or his close friends may accept to act as a mark of respect and affection for him and a duty to a departed loved one, when the trust is contained in a will. But some may not be so disposed. Professional trustees such as solicitors, banks and insurance companies will surely not accept to act unless they are paid.[25] But they cannot be paid unless the trust instrument contains a charging clause providing for the payment of the trustees. It is, therefore, advisable to have such a. clause in the trust instrument even when non-professionals are named as trustees particularly if the trust property is substantial.

Therefore, the rule that trustees must not be paid out of the trust property is subject to the following exceptions:

---

[24] S. 2(3)
[25] If the Public Trustee is appointed he is statutorily empowered to charge fees.

i) Trustees are entitled to recover their out-of-pocket expenses such as insurance premiums and agents fees paid by them.
ii) Trustees, whether professionals or non-professionals, are paid for their services if the trust instrument contains a *charge clause.*
iii) The public trustee is paid such fees as are fixed by Government order.
(iv) The court has power to order remuneration of a trustee in exceptional cases.[26]
(v) Trustees may contract for their remuneration with the beneficiaries who are of full age and capacity. This is not encouraged by the court because it may be one-sided and to the detriment of the beneficiaries as a whole.
(vi) The rule in *Craddock v Piper.*[27]

Like other trustees, a solicitor - trustee is prohibited from charging fees for his service to the trust. However, according to the rule a solicitor - trustee may charge costs if he acts for a co-trustee as *well as himself* in respect of business done in an action or matter *in court.* A solicitor-trustee may employ his *pat-trier* in cases where it would be proper to employ an outside solicitor and pay him proper charges out of the trust, provided that he himself would derive no benefit, direct or indirect, from such an employment.[28] This power is not restricted to matters in court but it does not enable a solicitor- trustee to employ his own firm.

Apart from the specific exceptional cases considered above, a trustee must not make a profit, directly or indirectly, from his management of the trust property. For example, if a trustee is appointed director in a company by virtue of the shares, which are part of the trust property, he must hold the director's fees paid on him to constructive trust for the trust. This is an illustration of the rule on constructive trust for the trust. This is an illustration of the rule in *Keech v Sandford.*[29]

A testator bequeathed a term of years to B on trust for an infant. Before the expiration of the term, B in his capacity as trustee, applied to the lessor to renew the lease for the befit of the infant. He refused, whereupon B took the lease for his own benefit. It was held that B held the renewed lease for the infant.

Trustees are under an obligation to distribute the trust property to the beneficiaries according to their entitlement as stipulated in the trust instrument. They have to carry out this function meticulously, because if they pay over to the wrong person, they would be personally liable for the amount. However,

---

[26] *Boardman* v *Phipps* (1965) Ch. 992
[27] (1850) 1 Mac & G 564
[28] *Clack* v *Carlon* (1861) 30 LJ Ch. 639
[29] (1726) Sel. Cas. King 61

rustees have quasi-contractual right to recover the amount of wrong payment from the recipient if his mistake is of fact but not if it is of law.[30]

An unpaid or under-paid beneficiary may, in addition to his right to sue the trustees, trace the trust property and recover it from the wrongfully paid recipient, unless the latter can show that he is a *bona fide* purchaser for value without notice of the breach of trust. Trustees may be relieved by the court from liability if they make erroneous distribution and it is shown that they acted honestly and reasonably and ought fairly to be excused.

In the process of carrying out their duties, the trustees may be confronted by problems, which they cannot easily resolve. In that sort of situation they are entitled to apply to the court for directions. So also if they have a doubt about the proper interpretation of the trust instrument; they may seek the assistance of the court. If they act consistently with the directions of the court on any matter, they would be shielded for liability.

Powers of trustees

In the foregoing pages, I considered the duties of trustees in the process of administering a trust. By its nature, a duty must be performed by the person upon whom it is imposed. He has no discretion as to whether or not to do so, for, it is obligatory. Therefore, failure by trustees to perform their duties results in a beach of the trust for which they are liable.

It is now proposed next to examine the power of the trustees. Trust instruments normally give express powers to them. Besides, a number of powers are conferred on them by statute and they are directed to exercise such powers in the absence of a contrary provision in the trust instrument. They are allowed to use their discretion in exercising the powers and the court will normally not interfere once they do so in accordance with their own judgment and in the best interest of the trust.

Specific powers

Trustees normally have the power to sell the trust property. This power is conferred by statute, but it is often given by the trust instrument expressly or by implication. If the property is land held on trust for sale, the trustees have, not just the power, but also the duty to sell, though they can postpone sale if they unanimously agree to do so. In carrying out the sale, they must endeavour to obtain the best price possible. If the price is inadequate the beneficiaries or any of them can proceed against the trustees.

---

[30] *Re Diplock* (1974) Ch. 716

After the conveyance of land to a purchaser the beneficiaries cannot effectively impeach his title unless such a purchaser colluded with the trustees to do an underhand deal.[31] The statute empowers trustees to insure any building or other insurable property up to 3/4 of the value of the property insured against fire. The premiums are paid out of the income of the property or of other property subject to the same trust.[32]

Wide discretion is given to trustees to deal with claims by or against the trust estate. They are empowered to compromise, compound, abandon any claim or submit the same to arbitration or otherwise settle any debt, account or other claims relating to the estate or pay or allow any debt or claim and accept a composition for any debt or for any property claim.[33]

Trustees being delegates of the donor, cannot themselves delegate their power. The principle is *delegates non potest delegare.* However, they may employ as agents, professionals such as solicitors, bankers, stockbrokers and insurance companies, in handling matters requiring special skill possessed by them. The trustees will not be liable for the default of such an agent, provided there is a need for the appointment and that they exercised proper care in selecting the agent for the particular assignment and closely supervised him. It is, for example, a wrong exercise of discretion to delegate the investment of trust funds to a solicitor who misapplied them.[34]

If a trustee is going to be out of the country for more than one month, he may by a power of attorney, delegate to any person, the execution or exercise during such absence, all or any trusts, powers or discretion.[35] The trustee may not appoint his sole co-trustee unless the latter is a trust corporation. However the trustee remains liable for the acts of the attorney as if they were his acts.

Trustees are empowered to pay trust money into court in exceptional circumstances.[36] Examples of situations that may warrant such an action are where it is uncertain to whom the money should be paid and where the beneficiaries are infants who cannot give a good discharge.

Control by the beneficiaries and the Court

In administering a trust, the trustees are guided by the term of the trust instrument, the statute and the principles of equity. They are not obliged to consult the beneficiaries nor accede to their wishes. The beneficiaries have no right o interfere in the trustees' exercise of their powers and duties. However, even though the beneficiaries are incompetent to interfere in the management of

---

[31] Trustee Act, s. 14; Trustee Law, s. 55(2)
[32] Trustee Act, s. 18; Trustee Law, s. 11
[33] Trustee Act, s. 21; Trustee Law, s. 7
[34] *Rowland* v *Witherden* (1851) 3 Mac & G. 568
[35] Trustee Law, s. 16(1)
[36] Trustee Act, s. 42; Trustee Law, s. 46

the trust while it is in existence, they can, if they are *sui juris* and are absolutely entitled to the trust property, unanimously put an end to the trust and compel the trustees to hand over the trust property to them. This is the well-known rule in *Saunders* v *Vautier*.[37] In this case there was a trust for the accumulation of funds for the benefit of a sole beneficiary until he was 25. He claimed the fund at 21 and this was sanctioned by the court.

The court exercises a general power of control over trustees and in this connection can issue directions and determine any question with respect to a trust. However, where the trustees have absolute discretion to execute a trust, the court will generally not interfere with the exercise of the discretion as long as they act in good faith.[38]

In the case of private trust the trustees may not exercise any *power* unless they are unanimous. If the majority desires to exercise a power the minority should not fall in line. In other words, the wishes of the minority will prevail. But if the trustees have a *duty* to perform an act, the court will intervene to compel the majority. Thus, if there is a trust for sale of land with power to postpone sale, the trust for sale must prevail even if the majority wants to postpone sale. Postponement is possible only if *all* the trustees agree.[39]

Finally, the court has no power to alter the terms of a trust however advantageous - such an action may be perceived to be for beneficiaries.[40] The only exception is that the court is empowered to authorize a departure from the terms of the trust if an emergency arises in the administration or management of the trust property, or in order to salvage the property. But the court cannot sanction a variation or an alteration of the beneficial interest.[41]

Conclusion

I have discussed in this chapter the nature of the trust concept, the appointment of trustees and the determination of such an appointment. The duties and powers of trustees were also examined. These discussions were undertaken against the background of legal regime regulating the trust institution. Special attention was drawn to some provisions, which could pose problems, and strategies, which could be employed to circumvent them.

The role of the court in the process of the administration of a trust was highlighted. The court has a general supervisory power in that process. As a general rule the trustees are allowed considerable latitude to administer the trust

---

[37] (1841) 4 Beav. 115
[38] *Gisborne* v *Gisborne* (1877) 2 App. Cas. 300
[39] *Re Hilton* (1901) Ch. 548
[40] *Re Walker* (1901) Ch. 879 at 885
[41] *Chapman* v *Chapman* (1954) AC 429 at 454/5

as they see fit, provided that they have due regard to the terms of the trust. Their discretion is normally not disturbed by the court once they appear to act in good faith and as prudent businessmen. The court, it must be noted, does not intervene *suo motu* but normally at the instance of the trustees or the court, which awards appropriate remedy in satisfaction of a proven case of infraction.

In all, it is my view that there is a reasonably adequate legal framework under which the trustees can carry out their mandate in pursuance of the wishes of the donor who instituted the trust. But the bottom line is the appointment of fit and proper persons to serve as original trustees and the provision in the trust instrument of adequate modalities for the appointment of new or additional trustees. Once this is done, then the chances are that the intention of the donor will substantially be met. Lawyers who are called upon to draft trust instruments will do well to bear this in mind.

Chapter 3

The standard duty of care of trustees

– Professor Musa Yakubu

In this chapter, I intend to discuss the *standard of skill* and *duty of care* of the trustees in relation to a trust property. Thus, matters like the nature of trust, the development of the law of trust, classification of trust, parties to a trust, kind of trusts, creation of trust, constructive trusts, appointments, removal and retirement of trustees, the trustees' powers, breach by trustees and determination of trustees' duties will be excluded from discussion. A trust imposes both legal and equitable obligations on a person described as a trustee in relation to the trust property, which is held and controlled by him for the benefit of the person(s) described as the beneficiaries.[1]

Trustees have a number of duties, which are imposed on them to protect the interests of the beneficiaries in the trust property and these are in the discourse.

Duty on the acceptance of the trust

On accepting a trust, the trustee is bound to ascertain the property comprised in the trust. To this end, the trustee shall examine all the relevant documents in order to ascertain the content of the trust. Thereafter, the duty of a trustee is properly to preserve the trust property, to pay the income or transfer the corpus to persons are entitled, to give all his *cestui que trust* account and information whenever demanded.[2] A trustee cannot assert a title of his own to trust property, nor divest himself of the trust property. If he ventures to deviate from the instrument of his appointment, he does so under the obligation and at the peril of afterwards satisfying the court that the deviation was necessary or beneficial to the terms of the trust. *Prima facie* a trustee must act personally, and as a general rule, a trustee sufficiently discharges his duty if he takes, in managing trust

---

[1] *Earl of Egmont* v *Smith* (1877) 6 ch. D 469
[2] *Re A Debtor* (1949) 1 All E.R. 510

affairs, the precautions which an ordinary prudent man of business would take managing similar affairs of his own.[3]

A trustee cannot be compelled to accept the office of trustee, but having accepted it, he must discharge its duties so long as his character as trustee subsists. The law does not recognize any distinction between active and passive trustees and a trustee will be fully liable to the *cestui que trust* for any loss that occurs, where he has left the management of the trust to a co-trustee. A trustee should ensure that legal title to the trust property is duly transferred to him in full.

Duty not to profit from the trust

Various authorities may be cited to illustrate the wide principle, continually re-stated that whenever a trustee being the ostensible owner of property acquires any benefits as the owner of that property, that benefit cannot be retained by him.[4] It is an inflexible rule of the Court of Equity that a person in a fiduciary position is not, unless otherwise expressly provided, entitled to make a profit; he is not allowed to put himself in a position where his interest and duty conflict.[5] The liability arises from the mere fact of profit having being made by the fiduciary. The profiteer, however honest and well-intentioned, cannot escape the risk of being called upon to account.

This general principle can be considered under the following:

Duty to act without remuneration

In the early days, it was an established rule that a trustee should have no allowance for his care and trouble in the administration of trust property. The rule does not, however, mean that there is necessarily anything illegal or improper in a trustee receiving remuneration, but the onus is on the trustee to point to a provision in the trust instrument or some rule of law, which establishes his right to remuneration. It is not that reward for services is repugnant to the fiduciary duty, but that he who has the duty shall not take any secret remuneration or any financial benefit not authorized by the law, or by his contract, or by the trust deed under which he acts.

A trustee, therefore, can only receive remuneration under the provisions of trust instrument, contract with *cestui que trust,* order of the court, statutory provisions, custom or remuneration under foreign practice.

---

[3] *Eaton* v *Budianan* (1911) AC 253 HL
[4] *Keech* v *Sandford* (1726) Sel. Cas. ch. 61
[5] *Bray* v *Ford* (1896) AC 44 Per Lord Herschell

Duty to account

The general rule is that "whenever a trustee, being the ostensible owner of property, acquires any benefit as the owner of that property, that benefit cannot be retained by himself, but must be surrendered for the advantage of those who are beneficially interested.[6] A trustee should keep accounts and be ready to produce them to the beneficiaries at any time. Thus, in *Re Francis,*[7] the trustees were required to account for remuneration, which they voted to themselves as directors by virtue of their holding of the trust shares. In *Re Macadam,*[8] the trustees had power by virtue of the articles of the company to appoint two directors of the company. They appointed themselves and were held liable to account for the remuneration they received for services as directors. Any payment made to a trustee to induce him to act in any particular way in connection with the trust business must be held by him as a trust fund. The reason for this rule is that the trustees have acquired the remuneration by the direct use of their trust powers.[9] As Cohen J observed,[10] "... the root of the matter is: Did the trustee acquire the position in respect of which he drew the remuneration by virtue of his position as trustee?"

Duty to give information

Beneficiaries are entitled to be informed about matters affecting their trust. In order to facilitate the supply of up to date information a trustee should keep a trust diary or minutes or recorded decisions and events affecting the trust.

A *cestui que* trust is prima facie, in the absence of special circumstances, entitled to production and inspection of all trust documents in the possession of the trustees. This includes title deeds and other documents relating to the title to the trust property and the nature and content of his own beneficial interest. He is also entitled to be given any necessary authority to verify the information given and to ascertain that the trust property is free from any encumbrances. The right to inspect the trust document is a proprietary right. The beneficiary is entitled to see all the trust documents because they are trust document and they are in a sense his own.

It is not, however, clear whether trustee's discretionary powers or dealings are bound to be disclosed to the beneficiaries. In Re *Londonderry's Settlement,*[11] the donees of a power under a discretionary trust decided to distribute the capital. One member was not happy with the sum intended to be

---

[6] See footnote 4 above.
[7] (1905) 92 LT 77
[8] (1945) 2 All ER 664
[9] *Archibong v Archibong*
[10] (1945) 2 All ER at 672
[11] *Tiger v Barclays Bank Ltd* (1952) 1 All ER 85

given to her. She, therefore, asked for copies of the minutes of the trustees' documents prepared for the meeting and correspondence between various interested beneficiaries and the trustees. The trustees were willing to show her only the documents giving the intended distribution and the annual trust accounts. They refused in the interest of the family or members' co-existence to disclose additional document.

They then brought summons in court for the purpose of determining the nature and extent of their duties. The court addressed itself firstly to what constituted trust documents. The court decided that there are three main characteristics of what constitutes trust document:

i)   They are documents in the possession of trustees as trustees;
ii) They contain information about the trust which the beneficiaries are entitled to know;
iii) The beneficiaries have proprietary interest in the documents and are accordingly entitled to see them.

The court may not order the disclosure of confidential information the disclosure of which may cause rift amongst the family or members, particularly, if the benefit to be derived from the disclosure is not much. It must also be noted that dealings with discretionary trust are confidential matters. Where *mala fide* is proved, however, in the exercise of discretionary trust, the court may order disclosure. It should also be noted that trustee's duty is not restricted to merely answering questions of the beneficiaries. It also includes giving information relating to the interests of the beneficiaries under the trust. Thus, an infant beneficiary is entitled on attaining majority age to be informed of his interests and entitlements in the trust.[12]

Trustees under an express trust are not only required to give information on demand, but when there is an infant beneficiary, are under a positive duty to inform him of his interest on his coming of age.[13]

Unjust enrichment or incidental profits

This is popularly known as the rule in *Keech* v *Sandford* under English Law. This occurs mainly under constructive trust. The rule simply is that a person may recover or regain title to that which has been unfairly withheld from him to the benefit of the withholder. The rule prevents a trustee from keeping to himself benefit, which would have gone to the beneficiary. Therefore, if profits come to a trustee in his capacity as such, he must hand them over to the beneficiary.

---

[12] (1965) Ch. 918
[13] *Hawkesley* v *May* (1956) 1 QB 304

Trustees who become directors by virtue of their trusteeships are liable to account for the remuneration they received because they acquired it by the use of their powers as trustees.

Trustees should not place themselves in positions where their duties and their interests conflict. Thus, a trustee shall not set up a business, which competes with his trust. In *Re Thompson,*[14] the executors of a will were directed to carry on the business of a testator who had been a yacht broker. One of the executors intended to set-up on his own account as yacht broker in competition. It was held that he could not set up the business. In the case of *Moore v Mglynn,*[15] is however, the facts are in *pari materia* with *Re Thompson,* the Court held that a trustee can set up a similar business on his own account as it stated:

> I have not been referred to nor am I aware of any case deciding that a trustee of a will carrying on the business of his testator is disabled from setting up a similar business in the locality on his own account. I am not prepared to hold that a trustee is guilty of a breach of trust in setting up for himself business in the neighbourhood.

It is, however, certain that where the trustee resorted to deception of solicitation of the customers of the other shop or business, in preference of his trust he may be held liable.

Not to purchase the trust property

A trustee and many other persons who occupy fiduciary positions are absolutely prohibited from purchasing the trust property. This is an inflexible rule of most general application and it is not founded upon any question of fraud on the part of the trustee. It is the logical consequence of the position, which the trustee occupies. This principle is illustrated by *Wright v Morgan*[16] wherein the trustee had acquired an option to purchase trust property at a valuation to be given by another trustee. It might have been thought that the independent valuation would have ensured a fair sale, but the Privy Council was of the opinion that the disability still existed, and moreover, the interests of the trustees as vendor and purchaser still conflicted in respect of selecting the moment of sale, which might obviously affect the price. This rule was further exhaustively examined and developed by Lord Eldon during his lengthy tenure of office as Lord Chancellor as he may be regarded as having placed the rule beyond possibility of serious limitation. Sir W. Grant M.R who followed Lord Eldon strictly had to consider

---

[14] *Re Utley* (1912) 106 LT 858
[15] (1930) 1 Ch. 203
[16] (1894) Irish Report, 74

the case of trustees who had purchased trust property at an auction. The Master of the Rolls said,

> the rule is a rule of general policy to prevent the possibility of fraud and abuse; for it may not always be possible to know whether the property was undersold.[17]

In another case,[18] Lord Eldon stated:

> This doctrine as to purchases by trustees, assignees and persons having a confidential character, stand much more upon general principle than upon the circumstances of any individual case. It rests upon this: that the purchase is not permitted in any case, however honest the circumstances; the general interests of justice requiring it to be destroyed in every instance as no court is equal to the examination and ascertainment of the truth in much the greater number of cases.

In *Aberdeen Railway Co. v Blakie Brothers*,[19] the House of Lords fully affirmed the breadth of the principle enunciated by Lord Eldon, and applied it to dealings between a director and his company. Lord Cranworth, L.C. therefore stated:

> A corporate body can only act by agent and it is, of course, the duty of those agents so to act as best to promote the interests of the corporation whose affairs they are conducting. Such agents have duties to discharge of a fiduciary nature towards their principal. And it is a rule of universal application that no one, having such duties to discharge, shall be allowed to enter into engagements in which he has or can have a personal interest conflicting or which possibly may conflict with the interests of those whom he is bound to protect. So strictly is this principle adhered to that no question is allowed to be raised as to the fairness or unfairness of a contract so entered into. It obviously is or may be impossible to demonstrate how far in any particular case the terms of such a contract have been the best for the interest of the *cestui que trust,* which it was possible to obtain. It may sometimes happen that the terms on which a trustee has dealt or attempted to deal with the estate or interests of those for whom he is a trustee, have been as good as could have been obtained from any other person - they may even at the time have been better. But still so inflexible is the rule that no inquiry on the subject is permitted. The English authorities on this head are numerous and uniform.

---

[17] (1926) AC 788
[18] *Lister v Lister* (1802) 6 Vers. 631. See also the Algerian case of *Khury v Jojo* (1956) WARL 102
[19] *Ex Parte James* (1803) 8 Vcs 337.

The court of Appeal in Nigeria in 1986 cited with approval the above statement of the general rule in England in *Okesiyi v Lawal*[20] to emphasize that the rule also applied in Nigeria *mutatis mutandis*. The rule applies to property of all kinds, whether real or personal, whether in possession or in reversion. The trustee may not sell to a person who is in fact a trustee for himself and all other circuitous arrangements to achieve the same result are equally invalid. A trustee for sale cannot lease to himself. A trustee cannot purchase on behalf of his children or friends or business associates. The rule applies to all persons who occupy a fiduciary position, although perhaps not with the same rigidity as to trustees.

Duty not to deviate

The fundamental principle is that a trustee must faithfully observe the directions contained in the trust instrument and as a rule, the court has no jurisdiction to give, and will not give its sanction to the performance by trustees of acts with reference to the trust estate which are not on the face of the instrument creating the trust, authorized by its terms.[21] The above statement is the general rule and the rule only. However, where there exists necessities or exigencies, the court may allow very limited exceptions. For example, where all the beneficiaries being of full age and capacity act together they can consent to what would otherwise be a breach of trust so as to free the trustees from the liability or indeed even to bring to an end the trust. Romer LJ in delivering the judgment in the case of *Re New* said,

> In the management of the trust estate.... It not frequently happens that some peculiar state of circumstances arises for which provision is not expressly made by the trust instrument and which renders it most desirable, and it may be even essential for that benefit of the estate and in the interest of all the *cestui que trust* that certain acts should be done by the trustees which in ordinary circumstance they would have no power to do. In a case of this kind, which may reasonably be supposed to be one not foreseen or anticipated by the author of the trust, where the trustees are embarrassed by the emergency that has arisen and the very duty cast upon them to do what is best for the estate and the consent of all the beneficiaries cannot be obtained by reason of some of them not being *sui juris* or in existence then it may be right for the court and the court in a proper case would have jurisdiction to sanction on behalf of all concerned such acts on behalf of the trustee.

---

[20] (1854) 1 Macq. 461
[21] (1986) 2 NWLR 417

It should be noted, however, that the jurisdiction is one to be exercised with great caution. The court takes care not to strain its powers. The court should not be justified in sanctioning an act simply for the sake of it's being desirable or beneficial to the beneficiaries or the estate.

Duty not to delegate the trust

Trustees who take on themselves the management of property for the benefit of others has no right to shift their duty on other persons. That means they have to do the work and actions personally. It was early realised that administration of trust would often be impracticable unless exception was permitted. The rule still remains that trustees have the duty to perform their functions personally. Trustees cannot delegate unless they have authority to do so.[22] Lord Hardwick said that trustees could "act by other land" on the ground of legal necessity or what he called moral necessity.[23] Thus, trustees acting according to the ordinary course of business and employing agents, as a prudent man of business would do on his behalf are not liable for the default of an agent so employed.

What this exception appears to say is: A, a Brazilian living in Brazil owns property in Lagos, which he obtained while doing business in Nigeria fifty years ago, he is now and leaving in Brazil, comes to Nigeria to get the property sold. He then appoints B, an estate agent, to act on her behalf to sell the estate. The appointment of B is legal. The administratrix is not liable for the default of B. This exception is reasonable otherwise the sale of the estate may be difficult and perhaps detrimental to the interest of the beneficiaries. The office of the trustee is one of personal confidence, and can, therefore, only be delegated in consequence of an express power contained in the trust instrument or of the statutory power. In appointing an agent the trustee must exercise his personal discretion in making his choice of agent. He cannot delegate the choice to someone such as his solicitor, though he may ask his opinion, advice or even names of suitably qualified persons to act for him. Thus, trustees may employ a broker for investment, solicitor for legal work, rent collector to collect rents. A trustee was held liable when he appointed a solicitor to invest a trust fund when the fund was misapplied.[24] It was held that it is not in the ordinary course of business for a solicitor to collect trust funds and invest them. This is just as if he has put the money into his pocket. A statute may allow a trustee to appoint an agent to administer the trust estate on his behalf.[25]

---

[22] (1901) 2 Ch. 534
[23] *Pilkington* v *I.R Cmoors* (1962) 3 All ER 622
[24] *Ex Parte Belchier* (1754) 218, *Dewar* v *Brooke* (1885) 52 LT 489
[25] S.23 Trustee Act, 1925. See also s. 14(1) Trustees Edict

Duty to act unanimously

Master of Rolls, Mr. Jessel once said, "there is no law that I am acquainted with which enables the majority of trustees to bind the minority."[26] The only action, which binds all the trustees, is the action of them all. Subject to a contrary provision in the trust instrument, only the joint exercise of power by the trustees will be valid. It is only a receipt by all the trustees will give a good discharge to a purchaser. The trust fund or estate should be under the joint control of all the trustees. If one trustee obtains control of some or the entire fund and misapplies it, his co-trustee will be fully liable.[27] They may, however, escape liability if they can show that the trustee properly obtained control of the fund and that the co- trustees acted promptly to get the money invested in their joint name. It also seems that trustees may not be liable for trust money obtained by a co-trustee without the knowledge of other trustees or consent and by fraud upon them.

Thus, the general rule is that all trustees must unanimously act in order to have a binding effect. If one of them takes action, it is presumed that all the rest have sanctioned the action and all are liable. The rest can only escape liability if it can be proved the other acted without authority or fraudulently. There is, therefore, duty upon the trustees to act unanimously.

Duty to hand over the trust property to the right persons

The obvious duty of the trustee in relation to the distribution of the trust property is to pay the proper persons. The trustee must ensure who are the persons to whom he must pay. Where the trustees know exactly the persons or beneficiaries of the trust property, there is no problem in identifying the persons entitled to the distribution or reversion of the trust property. But where the beneficiaries are not well known or identified, the persons entitled thereto must be ascertained. Accordingly, trustees have been held liable to the persons rightly entitled. Where they have paid the wrong persons through acting on a forged document, trustees will be held liable to pay if they ignore a derivative title of which they have notice whether actual or constructive.[28] Trustees have a right to call on anyone who claims to be a beneficiary to prove his title, but they cannot raise questions where the validity or invalidity of the doubt is not essential to their safety. Where the trustees have a reasonable doubt as to the title of the claimant, for instance, where he claims under an appointment which may be a fraud, a court may be called upon to verify or give direction.

---

[26] *Luke* v *Smith Kensington Hotel* (1879) 11 Ch. 121
[27] *Lewis* v *Nobbs* (1878) 8 Ch. D 591
[28] *Hallows* v *Lloyd* (1888) 29 Ch. D 686

Duty to invest the trust property

A trustee is under a duty to invest the trust property in his custody. The purpose of investing trust funds is to generate interest or income and also to maintain the capital. Equity generally requires from a trustee the same diligence as he showed in his own private affairs while dealing with other persons. In the case of investments of trust property, he is not allowed the same discretion. He may be prepared to take a risk for his personal benefit to secure a greater immediate return. As a trustee, he has a duty to preserve the trust fund or property for the benefit of persons entitled in succession. The trustees shall, therefore, avoid all hazardous enterprises even though included within the list of trustee investments.

In *Re Whiteley*,[29] Lindley L.J. stated: "The duty of a trustee is not to take such care only as a prudent man would take if he had only himself to consider; the duty rather is to take such care as an ordinary prudent man would take if he were minded to make an investment for the benefit of other people for whom he felt morally bound to provide."

This defers very fundamentally with principles of Islamic law. Under Islamic Law, unless the trust documents has expressedly directed for investment or the beneficiaries have directed the trustees to invest, trustees have been prohibited from investing trust property. The reason for this is that Islamic law regards every investment as being hazardous. There is no certainty of having the capital maintained not to talk of certainty in making profit. Thus, it is safer to keep the trust property in tact and sure of paying the beneficiaries. If the trust document has provided for investing the fund, it must also provide for the risk of that investment.

Duty to maintain equality

There is a duty on the trustees to make sure that all beneficiaries are treated according to the terms of the trust document. A trustee should not favour one beneficiary at the expense of another. Trustees should act impartially between all the beneficiaries.

---

[29] (1886) 33 Ch. D 347

Chapter 4

The uses of trusts in the management of property: *problem and prospects*

– Professor A .A. Utuama

Introduction

In legal jurisprudence, an owner of property has the right of its possession, use and enjoyment, management and control, among others.[1] He may decide to exercise these rights or any of them in person or through another. The institution of trust is easily the most important and curious device for the separation of the right of enjoyment from the right of management property of ever produced by English legal genius,[2] and introduce to our country following the reception of English doctrines of equity.

The modern trust was derived from the English feudal 'use', which was invented by the medieval lawyers in order to overcome the hardship of the common law rules which prevented land from being left by will and the heavy feudal burdens imposed on freehold tenants.[3] Thus, where A, a feudal tenant, wanted to evade the heavy burdens and services attached to his grant, he would transfer the land to those of his friends, B. C. and D. to the 'use' of his son, E. As far as the lord of the manor was concerned, B, C, and D were the legal owners. On A's death, no feudal dues were payable with respect to the land, because its legal ownership vested in his friends. If B or C subsequently died, there was no interruption of ownership since the property passed to D as a sole owner under the doctrine of survivorship, which applied at common law to joint tenants.

If B, C and D attempted to deal with the land in a manner incompatible with their obligations towards E, the courts of chancery would intervene on E's behalf. E would not, however, obtain any redress in the courts of common law

---

[1] See Fitzerald, P.J., *Salmond on Jurisprudence*, Sweet & Maxwell (ed.) (1986) pp. 246 - 247. *Abraham* v. *Olorunfunmi* (1991) 1 NWLR (P. 165) 53 at 74 - 75.
[2] See Keeton, G.W; "The Changing Conception of Trusteeship," in *Current Legal Problems*, 1980, p. 14.
[3] See Padfield, C.F., *Law*, Heinemann, London (1981), p. 248.

because their jurisdiction was limited to legal rights and the legal owners or owner.

As will be seen, A's friend, as *feofees* to uses, had only the bare legal title, while the real beneficial ownership was in A's son, E, the *cestui que* use.

The use grew in importance between the fifteenth and sixteenth centuries so much so that it was said in 1500 that the greater part of the land in England was held in use.[4] This led to the inevitable loss of considerable feudal dues to the Crown that in 1535 the Statute of Uses was passed to halt uses, or at least severely curtail them.[5] Uses had become, however, a well established practice that it could not be swept away by any legislative fiat. It, therefore, persisted and curiously revived as trust. The trust, however, became interestingly, a much more sophisticated and elastic institution than the Use had ever been[6] and, indeed, one of the most distinctive features of English Law.[7]

The trust as a legal term has been variously defined but it has been suggested that the attempt by *Lewin On Trusts* quoted herein below is probably the most comprehensive.[8]

> The word 'trust' refers to the duty or aggregate accumulation of obligations that rest upon a person described as trustee. The responsibilities are in relation to property held by him, or under his control. That property he will be compelled by a court in its equitable jurisdiction to administer in the manner lawfully prescribed by the trust instrument, or where there be no specific provision, written or oral, or to the extent that such provision is invalid or lacking, in accordance with equitable principles. As a consequence the administration will be in such a manner that consequential benefits and advantages accrue, not to the trustee, but to the persons called *cestui que* trust or beneficiaries, if there be any; if not, for some purpose which the law will recognize and enforce. A trustee may be a beneficiary, in which case advantages will accrue in his favour to the extent of his beneficial interest.

The trust has become so developed and flexible that it is now being used for a wide variety of purposes, ranging from family settlement to environmental protection.[9] The object of this chapter is to highlight the principal uses of trust as a vehicle for managing property, examine the problems and prospects associated with its use today in our society.

---

[4] See Pettit, PH, *Equity and the Law of Trust*, 6th Ed., Butterworths (1989) p.12.
[5] Ibid.
[6] Ibid. Padfield, C.P, *op. cit.*, 249
[7] Ibid.
[8] Moffat, G., *Trusts Law, Text and Materials*, Butterworths, London (1994) p.3.
[9] See Oakley, J., Parker and Mellows, *The Modern Law of Trust*, 6th Ed., Sweet &Maxwell, London, (1994) pp. 3 - 4.

Principal uses

As noted above, the trust is serving in many fields and in our country, it is being used for several purposes, namely, to (i) enables property to be held for infants, (ii) create settlements, (iii) provision for dependants, (iv) facilitate the management of concurrent interest in property, (v) advance endowment and gifts for charitable purposes, (vi) provide pensions for retired employees, (vii) enable unincorporated association to hold property and (viii) vehicle for capital accumulation and doing business.

(i) To overcome the incapacity of infants to hold land

The legal title cannot be vested in an infant. There is no objection however to land being held upon trust for an infant. Section 7(a) of the Land Use Act, has adopted this principle. It states:

> It shall not be lawful for the Military Administrator to grant a statutory right of occupancy or consent to occupancy to a person under the age of twenty-one years:
> Provided that
> (a) Where a guardian or trustee for a person under the age of 21 has been duly appointed for such purpose, the Military Administrator may grant or consent to occupancy to such guardian or trustee on behalf of such person under age.

(ii) Settlement

A settlement means any deed, will, agreement or other instrument under or by virtue of which any property is or is deemed to be limited to or in trust for any person by way of succession. [10]

Thus, "a gift of property to A for life with remainder to his son" or gift of property on trust for A for life with remainder to his son" would create a settlement.

However, under the property and conveyancing law, operating in Oyo, Ogun, Ondo, Osun, Ekiti, Edo and Delta States, it is no longer possible to ensure that the person ultimately entitled will receive the very property that is settled, for the trustees who invariably have the power to sell the property, may decide to do so and re-invest the proceeds. As will be see later, it is possible to ensure that the beneficiaries receive either the property itself or the benefit of the investment.

---

[10] See Section 2 of the Settled Land Act of 1882; Section 2 of the Property and Conveyancing Law Cap 99 Laws of Oyo State; *Lady Alakija* v. *National Bank Nigeria Ltd.* 1974, CC HCJ/5/74, 649.

(iii) Unpublicised provision for dependants

A man who has broken his marriage vows of 'one man and one wife', to the exclusion of others and alongside maintains an enduring love affair outside his matrimonial home may, would usually wish to make provision for his mistress or any issue of the relationship. During his lifetime, there is hardly any problem. However, if a man provides for a mistress or children outside wedlock by will, the rat may be let out of the bag. As soon as probate has been obtained, the will becomes a public document and it is open to inspection. In *Johnson & Anor* v. *Maja*,[11] the testator's will, it will be recalled, was challenged on the ground, among others, that the execution was obtained by the undue influence of a woman who was the mistress of the testator. Although the attack on the will was unsuccessful, it gave undue publicity to the relationship between the testator and his mistress.

The *inter vivos* transfer of property on trust particularly, by means of secret trust will escape adverse publicity of this sort.

(iv) Protection of family property

A person may feel that an outright gift of money or property to a surviving spouse or child will lead to its dissipation. A gift of that money or property to trustees to hold upon trust to pay either the income or only a limited proportion of the capital to the surviving spouse or child will protect such property from wastrels and it will be preserved if the beneficiary goes bankrupt. The protective trust is a useful device for this purpose. In the words of Adigun in his invaluable book,[12]

> The owner of property can create beneficial interest under a trust and deny to the recipient of such interest both the power to alienate such interest and liability to have such unreachable by the creditors of such recipient. It is called the protective trust. The conveyancer can couch a protective trust in such terns that the creditors of a bankrupt are precluded from laying hand on the debtor's property although he is till indirectly enjoying the benefits of the trust.

(v) Enabling an association to hold property

Unincorporated associations, such as societies, clubs, trade unions, churches, mosques and nongovernmental organizations (N.G.O) and communities present anomalous conception for being unincorporated society. Although an

---

[11] (1951) 13 WACA 290.
[12] Adigun, *On Cases and Texts on Equity, Trusts and Administration of Estates*, Ayo Sodimu (1987) p. 254.

unincorporated association is not a separate entity in law from its members, it often has a continuing entity and yet it is not regarded and treated as the aggregate of its members. It cannot hold title to, or interest in land. It is against this background that a gift to the individual members of the association for the prosecution of its object, presents difficulty of construction in order to validate such a gift.[13] This gap and the attendant conveyancing difficulties have been abridged by statutory requirement of registration and incorporation of associations. This was first achieved under the Land Perpetual Succession Act[14] and now under Part C. of Companies And Allied Matters Act.[15] A basic principle of the Act is that upon an association being registered, the trustee or trustees shall become a corporate body in accordance with the provisions of Section 679 of the Act. The consequences flowing from Section 679 include the facts that the trustee or trustees have perpetual succession, power to sue and be sued in its corporate name and as such the trustees, subject to the directions of the association or of the council, or governing body, can hold and acquire, and transfer, assign or otherwise dispose of any property or interest therein belonging to, or held for the benefit of such association.

Thus behind the hedge of trustees, a community life or unincorporated associations may flourish in the furtherance of desired purposes. Secondly, the problem of endowments and of gifts for charitable, religious, educational, literary scientific, social, development, cultural or sporting is made easy, for the property may now be more conveniently and securely vested in trustees for such purposes as the settlor desires.[16]

(vi) Management of concurrent interests

One area in which the machinery of trust has been lavishly applied is in the administration of group interests within the jurisdiction of the property and conveyancing law. Under this law, land, held under a tenancy in common or joint tenancy is made subject to a "trust for sale." In Section 2 therein, a trust for sale is defined as "an immediate binding trust for sale, whether or not exercisable at the request or with the consent of any person, and with or without a power at discretion to postpone the sale." Although the law imposes an immediate trust, there is an implied power on the part of the trustees to postpone the sale indefinitely free from liability, the exercise of the power of sale may be subject to the consents of named persons, and the court under section 28 may exercise its jurisdiction to order or refuse to order a sale at the instance of an interested person. Although the basic theory of the property and conveyancing

---

[13] Pettit, P.H., *op. cit.*, pp.51 -52.

[14] Cap. 98 LFNL. 1958.

[15] Cap. 59, LFN, 199.

[16] See Paton, G.W. & Derham, D, (ed), *A Text Book of Jurisprudence*, 4th edition, Oxford (1972) p. 530.

law is to facilitate the process of land transfer with particular reference to concurrent interests and have the proceeds shared among the beneficiaries, the exercise of the power may be impeded by the presence of control mechanisms and bring the strange consequence of making the land incapable of sale.

(vii) Advancement of endowment and charitable purposes

It is generally accepted that government alone cannot be the sole agent of development and promoter of social security. Where this is the case the society as a whole will be the poorer for it. The wealthy members of society must be encouraged to plough back some portions of their excess resources into society through works of charity to complement public efforts. The trusts for charity provide the facility for the wealthy and philanthropist to settle property either by expenditure of capital or by retention of capital and expenditure of income to the advancement of those socially beneficial charitable objects. These were long ago classified by Lord Mcnaghten in *Commissioner for Special Purposes of Income Tax* v. *Pemsel*[17] into trusts for the relief of poverty, trusts for the advancement of education, trusts for the advancement of religion, and trusts for other purposes beneficial to the Community.

These trusts assist in giving material content to the economic, social and educational objectives embodied under the Fundamental Objective and Directive Principles of State Policy under the 1979 constitution as amended. So also will they give practical meaning to the fundamental right to dignity of human person, right to private and family life, right to freedom of thought, conscience and religion as well as the right of freedom of expression and the press enshrined under the same constitution for the class of beneficiaries concerned in particular and the society in general.

The alternative to trusts for charitable purposes is the establishment of a corporation having charitable objects such as a foundation for the relief of poverty, advancement of education or community development.

(viii) Scheme of pensions for employees

The need for both employer and employees to make provision for loss of income following voluntary or involuntary retirement for the latter for their support and those of their families and dependants cannot be overemphasized. There is the gratuity and pension scheme under the Pensions Act[18] for retired public servants. The National Provident Fund (NPF)[19] now known as Nigerian Social Insurance Trust Fund and other private and voluntary schemes exist for workers in the

---

[17] (1891) A.C. 531 at 583.
[18] CAP 346, Laws of the Federation, 1990.
[19] CAP 273, Laws of the Federation, 1990.

private sector. The private schemes may include the use of trust under a Trust Deed or trust corporations, such as NIDB Trustees Ltd. The fund contributed either by the employer alone or both the employer and the employees[20] is vested in the trustees with the objective of assuring the employee/beneficiary that his pension will in fact be forthcoming as and when due without recourse to his employer.

Apart from the provision of pensions trusts may be used to give incentive to employees out of profit beyond payment of wages. Such a scheme may be recognized in the form of trusts for the purchase of shares in the employing enterprise. From the case law, the discretionary trust[21] can be a useful device for achieving this goal.

ix. Vehicle for capital accumulation and doing business

In the business climate today, there is the dire need to raise capital for business investment from members of the public in return for interests or dividends. The trust has been a virile vehicle towards this end through the media of the debenture trust deed, unit trust and investment trust. The Company and Allied Matters Act[22] authorizes a company to borrow money for purposes connected with its business and execute as security a debenture trust deed appointing trustees for the debenture holders.

Section 186(2) imposes a specific duty on trustees to safeguard the right of the debenture holders and, on behalf of and for the benefit of them to execute the right powers and discretions conferred upon them by the trust deed.

Unit trust schemes are another vehicle by which companies may access public funds for investment purpose. Before the advent of the Investment and Securities Act (ISA) No.45 of 1999, unit trust schemes were regulated by sections 575 to 589 of the Companies and Allied Matters Act No. 1 of 1990. These provisions enabled the pooling of fund resources of small investors entrusted to a manger for the purpose of enabling the investors acquire a stake in a large portfolio of investments and in the vein distributing the risks of the investments across a substantial range of stocks and shares.

The funds so entrusted to the manager of the unit trust are invested in the stock market and the investments are vested in trustees, who by law must be a trust corporation, for the stakeholders. The trustees receive the dividends on the investments and after the deduction of costs of administration; the net is divided among the unit holders of the scheme.

---

[20] See Nwabueze, B.O., *Social Security in Nigeria*, Institute of Advanced Legal Studies (1989) p. 29.
[21] See *Re Gulbenkian* (1968) 1 ch. 126; *Re Baden Deed Trusts* (1969) 2 Ch. 388, C.A.
[22] Cap 59 Laws of the Federation, 1990. See sections 166, 183-188 thereof.

The provisions of the Companies and Allied Matters Act dealing with unit trust schemes have been repealed by ISA[23] and replaced by Sections 124 to 145 of the Act.

The essential advantages of the unit trust scheme include the following:

a) The cost of acquiring and managing the investment portfolio by the manager is proportionately less than the cost, which a unit holder would invariably incur if he were to proceed as an individual to acquire and manage an equivalent trust portfolio of investment instruments;

b) the manager or operator of the unit is usually an informed professional on investment matters or at least has access to expert advice and therefore is in a better position to take sound business decisions on investment than hopeful unit holder could;

c) by spreading investment across a range of investment instruments, the risk of loss of investment is reduced considerably; and

d) units are financially liquid assets capable of being redeemed at any time at the election of the unit holder.[24]

Essentially, the Investment and Securities Act requires that the business of a unit trust can only be carried out by a public limited liability company[25] registered with the Securities and Exchange Commission with a minimum paid-up capital N20,000,000.[26] The trustees appointed are a body corporate such as a bank or insurance company or corporate trustee like NIDB Trustees licensed under the relevant statute and having a minimum paid-up capital of N40,000,000[27] and the power of investment limited to the securities approved by the Commission from time to time. The holder of a unit trust may redeem its unit at the price for the time being at which the manager buys units of the scheme.[28] It is pertinent to note that the manager does not in fact have power to determine the price at which he may buy units. Unit prices are determined by the Securities and Investment Commission in accordance with a formula laid down in its Rules and Regulations.[29]

The community oriented schemes such as *Esusu* have now been given statutory backing.

The foregoing list of uses of the trust vehicle is by no means exhaustive and will continue to grow. Future demands will undoubtedly stimulate the

---

[23] See sections 261 and 263
[24] Section 131(1) ISA
[25] Section 22 and 26 thereof; *Savannah Bank (Nig.) Ltd.* v *Ajilo* (1989) 1 NWLR (pt 97/ 305.
[26] Section 125(3)(b) ISA
[27] Section 125(3)(c)
[28] Section 131(1)
[29] SEC Rules and Regulations, Rule 249 (see Schedule VI of the Rules)

development of other types of trust, such as *esusu*.[30] This should not alter, in any way, its central rule of one person being the property owner for the benefit of others. Thus, although the trust is a flexible instrument for management of property, the rules, which govern it, are by and large the same whatever the purpose for which it is employed.[31]

Problems and prospects

In spite of the very sophistication and dynamism of the trust, it is like any human device is not always imperfect in application. This may be due to the inherent weakness of the trust, the conversion of social values necessary for its application or its misuse. The ensuing discourse will highlight some of the peculiar difficulties, which the execution of trusts face in our jurisdiction and the prospects for overcoming them. The difficulties facing the application of trusts in our society may be classified into problems of (i) finding the right person as trustees, (ii) perfecting the creation of a trust, (iii) heavy cost of administration, (iv) trust under a will and (v) prescribed areas of investments.

(a) Problem of finding a suitable person to act as a trustee

The creation of a trust is premised on the availability of a person in whom the settlor or testator reposes confidence. Thus, it has been rightly suggested by a learned author that the conceptual starting-point of a trust is confidence reposed in some other.[32] Therefore the person to be appointed a trustee must command the respect of the appointor in terms of having the required disposition of character, of honesty, ability, and having good judgment in the management of his own affairs.

Writing the appraisal of the eighteenth century trustee, Keeton states:

> The typical trustees of the eighteen century, it has been suggested, was the country landowner, who managed his estate thriftily, stood high in the estimation of the country and almost certainly took his place upon the Bench at Quarter sessions.

Admittedly, there have been tremendous social changes in our time and society. The qualities of a trustee of the eighteenth century will now fit more of a successful professional or member of some well-established firm who sits

---

[30] Section 146 of ISA

[31] See generally Regulations 240–249 of SEC Rules and Regulations. See also sections 126-144 of ISA.

[32] LFN 1990, Paling, D., "Trustee Investment in a time of Economic Depression," in *The Conveyancer* Vol. 39, p. 321.

upon one or two boards of directors. A man who in spite of high position in society has considerable time and skill to devote to the gratuitous administration of the property of a neighbour, friend or relation. He may in the course be prepared to incur heavy legal liability if his judgement proved erroneous.

Today, in our country, it is becoming increasing difficult to find persons of this exceptional ability and standing to undertake the management of private trusts, under the heavy burden of the complexity of modern life in a depressed economy. For that reason the Public Trustee Law of Lagos State, for instance, has given a general power to a public trustee to delegate professional aspects of the business of the trust to relevant professionals for a fee for their services and for whom, the trustee is not legally responsible. Again, the era of the gratuitous private trustee is fast disappearing. The solicitor versed in legal knowledge will appear to be of first preference and importance. He has the advantage of the personal knowledge of the settlor and beneficiaries. Next will be the trust corporation. It has the advantage of security, perpetuity and the availability of pool of experts in its employment to handle the business of the trust. But such professional services can hardly be rendered free of charge. Any remuneration for the trustee will be extra administrative cost for the trust. In thinking of creating a private trust, the most probable candidate for appointment will be a solicitor or a trust corporation.

(ii) Problem of perfecting a trust

A fundamental principle in the constitution of *inter vivos* trust, is that the prospective settlor who intends to set up a trust by transferring property to a trustee must pass the legal title to the trustee depending on the nature of the property. For example, in the case of personal chattels capable of passing by delivery, there must either be delivery or a deed of gift, in case of and registered shares there must be instrument of transfer. With respect to land there must be an instrument on which the requisite consent has been endorsed under the Land Use Act. The strictness of this rule is underlined by the famous observation of Turner L.J in *Milroy* v. *Lord* when he said:

> I take the law of this court to be well settled that, in order to render a voluntary settlement valid and effectual, the settlor must have done everything which according to the nature of the property comprised in the settlement was necessary to be done in order to transfer the property and render the settlement binding upon him..... in order to render the settlement binding, one or other of these modes must as I understand the law of this court, be resorted to, for there is no equity in this court to perfect an, imperfect gift...If it is intended to take effect by transfer, the court will not hold the intended transfer to operate as a declaration of trust, for then every imperfect instrument would be made effectual by being converted into a perfect trust.

As has become fairly familiar, a transfer of the legal interest in a right of occupancy under the Land Use Act must be with the prior consent of the Governor of a State; otherwise it is rendered null and void. In view of the difficulty and expense of obtaining the requisite consent for the alienation of a right of occupancy, the creation of *inter vivos* trust of right of occupancy by transfer of the legal title to the intended trustee appears to be an arduous task. The decision of the Supreme Court in the subsequent case of *Awojugbagbe Light Industries Ltd.* v. *Chinukwe & NIDB Trustees* that an agreement to alienate or an instrument delivered as an escrow is not invalidated by the provisions of the Act but takes effect as an inchoate transaction until consent is procured, provides no solution to the problem. Because as was emphasized in *Milroy* v. *Lord* (*supra*) the court cannot perfect an imperfect gift. Given this difficulty, it is submitted that a holder of a right of occupancy intending to create an *inter vivos* trust of it, must begin early in time to seek the requisite consent and to meet the expenses thereof. There is little doubt that this will increase the cost of constituting a trust of land. Thus, it will be easier and less expensive to create a trust of chattels such as shares as well as choses-in-action.

(iii) Heavy cost of administration

As noted above, the era of gratuitous administration of trust appears to be drawing to an end. Remunerations have to be paid to trustees and their agents engaged by them to handle the different aspects of the trust business. Returns to investment by private trust attract tax under section 1 (b) of the Personal Income Tax Decree No. 104 of 1993 (PITD). Similarly, gains accruing from the trust property is taxable at rate of 10% under sections 1 and 2 of the Capital Grains Tax Act as amended. However, a charitable trust is exempted from taxation at the end of the day, except for the charitable trust, a private trust may not be an effective instrument of tax avoidance. Therefore, the impact of remuneration and taxation on private trust may make it unattractive. Hence, persons who wish to use trust for tax avoidance, will better be advised to constitute charitable trusts.

(iv) Trust under a will

A trust of property created by a will is favoured by the rules of perfect creation. It will not normally fail on the ground that it is incompletely constituted.[33] However, the validity and enforceability of a trust declared by a will depend, in the first place, on the validity and successful grand of the probate of the will.[34]

---

[33] Pettit, P. H., *op. cit.* p. 84
[34] See *Finnegan* v *Cementation Co. Ltd.* (1953) 1 QB 688 at 693. Mowbray, J.Q.C., "Trusts in Wills: Cross-Border Questions" in *International Legal Practitioner*, June 1998, p. 56

Thus, a testamentary trust is open to the question of the essential validity and effect of particular devise of the will.

(v) Prescribed areas of investments

The investments that a trustee can make are listed by the Trustee Investments Act as follows:[35]

(a) all securities hereafter created or issued by or on behalf of the Government of the Federation;

(b) securities hereafter created or issued by or on behalf of the Government of a State which are declared by the President by notice in the Federal Gazette to be securities to which this Act applies;

(c) securities which are declared by the president by notice in the Federal gazette to be securities in which this Act applies, being securities created or issued by companies or corporations incorporated directly by an Act enacted by the National Assembly or by a Law enacted by the House of Assembly of a State having effect as if it were so enacted which companies or corporations are specified in the Schedule hereto or which may be added to such Schedule by the president by notification in the Federal Gazette.

(d) debentures and fully paid-up shares of any company incorporated by and registered under the Companies and Allied Matters Act (other than a private company within the meaning of that Act).

The need to regulate the investments powers of a trustee had long been recognised. Since the South Sea Company in 1720, the categories of investments that a trustee can make have been fixed as a means of protecting beneficiaries from the vagaries of an uncertain economic situation. If the need was felt in England as long ago as the eighteen century, it is submitted that the issue is of greater concern in our country in view of the recent experience of the collapse pf many banks and financial institutions leading to loss of billions of investment. This notwithstanding, it is submitted that the list of authorised investment appears rather restrictive especially in respect of investment trusts.

The settlor and trustee are left without any discretion in the choice of investment portfolio. There are other safe and lucrative investment portfolios in the economy to which trust funds can be applied by a prudent trustee.

There is the need to widen the list of authorised securities, particularly with respect to trust corporations, with the principal object of carrying out trust business.

It is reasonable enough to expect the beneficiary to be protected by the general duty of skill and care imposed upon trustee.[36] The courts should be able

---

[35] Section 2(1)

to inquire in each case, whether, in selecting the particular investment, at the time and place when he did, the trustee was exercising the skill and care.[37]

Conclusion

The subject of discussion is a very large one and dealing with it in a very small compass as we have done here may not have given sufficient insight to the issues examined. But the main purpose of our effort has been to highlight some of the many uses a trust can be put into. Those examined do not in anyway exhaust the actual and potential uses of trust in our jurisdiction. But they may be sufficient to demonstrate the sophistication and enormous capacity of the trust to accommodate changing demands without its central rule as a means by which a person owns land for the benefit of others being altered.

It should be noted that the use of trust in the management of property is not free from problems. Happily, however, to every of such problem there is a prospective solution. Overall, the trust remains a unique and robust instrument for the settlement of settlor's family and dependants during his lifetime; capital accumulation and investments as well as the advancement of works of charity and community development.

---

[36] Sections 188 and 584 of Companies and Allied Matters Act, Cap. 59

[37] LFN 1990, Paling, D., "Trustee Investment: In a Time of Economic Depression", in *The Conveyancer*, Vol. 39, p. 321.

Appendix

CHAPTER 162

PUBLIC TRUSTEE LAW

A Law to provide for the appointment of a Public Trustee and to amend the law relating to the administration of trusts.

[12th October, 1960]

1. This Law may be cited as the Public Trustee Law.

2. In this Law unless the context otherwise require –

"court" means the High Court;

"expenses" includes costs and charges;

"Federal Public Trustee" means the federal authority empowered to administer trusts;

"letters of administration" means letters of administration of the estate and effects of a deceased person, whether general or with a will annexed, or limited either in time or of otherwise;

"lunatic" includes every persons adjudged a lunatic under the provision of the Lunacy Law and every person with regard to whom it is proved to the satisfaction of the court that such person is through mental infirmity arising from disease or age incapable of managing his affairs;

"private trustee" means a trustee other than the Public Trustee.

"trust" includes an executorship or administratorship, guardianship of infants, or the office of committee or receiver of the estate of any person incapable of managing his own affairs; and "trustee" shall be construed accordingly;

"trust property" includes all property in the possession or under the control wholly or partly of the Public Trustee by virtue of any trust.

Establishment of Public Trustee

3. (1) The office of Public Trustee is hereby created.

(2) The Public Trustee shall be a corporation sole under that name. With perpetual succession and an official seal, and may sue and be sued under the above name like any other corporation sole, but any instrument sealed by him shall not, by reason of his using a seal, be rendered liable to a higher stamp duty than if he were an individual.

4. (1) There may from time to time be appointed a fit person to the office of Public Trustee and such office may be held in conjunction with any other office, which the civil service Commission of Lagos State may approve.

(2) There may also be appointed such persons to be officers of the Public Trustees as are considered necessary for the purposes of this Law.

5. The person appointed to the office of Public Trustee shall be entitled to appear in court in person in any proceedings, which the Public Trustee is a party.

Powers and Duties of Public Trustee

6. (1) Subject to and in accordance with the provisions of this Law and the regulations made hereunder, the Public Trustee may, if he thinks fit –
   (a) act as an ordinary trustee;
   (b) act as a custodian trustee;
   (c) be appointed trustee by the court.

(2) Subject to the provision of this Law and the regulations made hereunder, the Public Trustee may act either alone or jointly with any person or body of person in any capacity to which he is appointed in pursuance of this Law, and shall have all the same powers, duties and liabilities, and be entitled to the same right and immunities and be subject to the control and orders of the court as a private trustee, committee or receiver acting in the same capacity.

(3) The Public Trustee may decline, either absolutely or except on the prescribed conditions, to accept any trust, but he shall not decline to accept any trust on the ground only of the small value of the trust property.

(4) The Public Trustee shall not accept any trust which involve the management or carrying on of any business, except in the cases in which he is authorised to do so by regulations made under this Law, nor any trust under a deed of arrangement for the benefit of creditors nor the administration of any estate known or believed by him to be insolvent

7. The Public Trustee may accept trusts, which are exclusively for religious or charitable purpose.

Public Trustee as Custodian Trustee

8. *(1) Subject to regulations under this Law, the Public:* Trustee may, if he consents to act as such, and whether or not the number of trustees has been reduced below the original number, be appointed to be custodian trustee of any trust -

(a) by order of the court made on the application of any person on who application the court may order the appointment of a new trustee; or

(b) by the testator, settlor, or other creator of any trust; or

(c) by the person having power to appoint new trustee.

(2) Where the Public Trustee is appointed to be custodian trustee of any trust -

(a) the trust property shall be transferred to the custodian trustee as if he were sole trustee, and for that purpose vesting order may, where necessary, be made by the court.

(b) the management of the trust property and the exercise of any power or discretion exercisable by the trustees under the trust shall vested in the trustees other than the custodian trustee (which trustees are hereinafter referred to as the managing trustees);

(c) as between the custodian trustee and the managing trustees, and subject and without prejudice to the right of any other persons, the custodian trustee shall have the custody of all securities and documents of title relating to the trust property, but the managing trustees shall have free access thereto and be entitled to take copies thereof or extracts therefrom;

(d) the custodian trustee shall concur in and perform all acts necessary to enable the managing trustees to exercise their powers of management or any other power or discretion vested in them (including the power to pay money or securities into court), unless the matter in which he is requested to concur is a breach of trust, or involves a personal liability upon him in respect of calls or otherwise, but, unless he so concurs, the custodian trustee shall not be liable for any act or default on the part of the managing trustees or any of them;

(e) all sums payable to or out of the income or capital of the trust property shall be paid to or by the custodian trustee:

Provided that the custodian trustee may allow the dividends and other income derived from the trust property to be paid to the managing trustees or to such person as they direct, or into such bank to the credit of such exonerated from seeing to the application thereof and shall not be answerable for any loss or misapplication thereof;

(f) the power of appointing new trustees, when exercisable by the trustees, shall be exercisable by the managing trustees alone, but the custodian trustee shall have the same power of applying to the court for the appointment of a new trustee as any other trustee;

(g) in determining the number of trustee for the purpose of any enactment, the custodian trustee shall not but reckoned as a trustee;

(h) the custodian trustee, if he acts in good faith, shall not be liable for accepting as correct and acting upon the trustees, as to any birth, death, marriage, or other matter of pedigree or relationship, or, other matte of fact, upon which the title to the trust property of any part thereof may depend, nor for acting upon any legal advice obtained by the managing trustees independently of the custodian trustee;

(i) the court may, on the application of either the custodian trustee, or any of the managing trustees, or of any beneficiary, and on proof to their satisfaction that it is the general wish of the beneficiaries, or that on other grounds it is expedient, to terminate the custodian trusteeship make an order for that purpose, and the court may thereupon make such vesting orders and give such directions as in the circumstances may seem to the court to be necessary or expedient.

(3) The provision of this section shall apply in like manner as to the Public Trustee to any banking or insurance company or other body corporate entitled by regulations made under this Law to act as custodian trustee, with power for such company or body corporate to charge and retain or pay out of the trust property fees not exceeding the fees chargeable by the Public Trustee as custodian trustee.

Public Trustee as an Ordinary Trustee

9. (1) The Public Trustee may be that name, or any other appointment sufficient description, be appointed to be trustee of any will of Public or settlement or other instrument creating a trust or to perform any trust or duty belonging to a class which he is authorised by regulations made under this Law to accept, and may be so appointed whether the will or settlement or instrument creating the trust of duty was made or came into operation before or after the commencement of this Law and either as an original or as a new trustee, or as an additional trustee, in the same cases, and in the same manner, and by the same persons or court, as if he was a private trustee, with this addition, that, thought the trustees originally appointed were two or more, the Public Trustee may be appointed sole trustee.

(2) Where the Public Trustee has been appointed a trustee of any trust, a co-trustee may retire from the trust notwithstanding that there are not more than two trustees.

(3) The Public Trustee shall not be so appointed either as a new or additional trustee where the will, settlement or other instrument creating the trust or duty contains a direction to the contrary, unless the court otherwise order.

(4) Notice of any proposed appointment of the Public Trustee, either as a new or additional trustee, shall, where practicable, be given in the prescribed manner to all persons beneficially interested who are resident in Nigeria and whose address are known to the person proposing to make the appointment, or, if such beneficiaries are infants, to their guardians.

(5) If any person to whom such notice has been given within twenty-one days from the receipt of the notice applies to the court, the court may, if having regard to the interest of all the beneficiaries it considers it expedient to do so, make an or prohibiting the appointment being made:

Provided that a failure to give any such notice shall not invalidate any appointment made under this section.

10. (1) Whether the Public Trustee is or not appointed a committee or receiver of a lunatic, he may apply to the court to direct a settlement of the property of a lunatic under this section

(2) Upon such application, the court may direct a settlement to be made of the property of a lunatic, or any part thereof of any interest therein, on such trusts and subject to such powers a provision as the court may deem expedient, and in particular may give such directions -

(a) Where the property has been acquired under a settlement, a will or an intestacy, or represents property so acquired; or

(b) Where by reason of any change in the law of intestacy or of any change circumstances since the execution by the lunatic of a testamentary disposition, or of any absence of information at the such execution, or on account of the former management of the property or the expenditure of money in improving or maintaining the same or for any other special reason the court is satisfied that any person might suffer an injustice if the property were allowed to devolve as undisposed of on the death intestate of the lunatic or under any testamentary disposition executed by him.

(3) The court may direct the committee or receiver of the lunatic or any trustee for him, to execute any trust instrument, conveyance or other instrument, and to do any other act or thing which may be required for giving effect to the settlement, in the name and on behalf of the lunatic and, for that purpose, may make a vesting order or appoint a person to convey; and any settlement approved by the court shall be as effectual and binding on all persons interested as if the same had been made by the lunatic while of full capacity.

(4) This section applies whether or not the lunatic has executed a testamentary disposition and notwithstanding that it is not known whether he has executed such a disposition or not, but does not apply when he is an infant.

(5) (a) Any person who under any enactment for the time being in force relating to the administration of property has a *spes successionis* (whether under any testamentary disposition which is known to exist or in the event of the intestacy of the lunatic) or an interest in the property of the lunatic or in any part thereof, as well as the committee or receiver and any other person may request the Public Trustee to apply to the court under this section and if the Public Trustee shall neglect or refuse so to do, such person may himself apply to the court under this section provided that notice of his application shall be served on the public Trustee who may appear upon the hearing of the application.

(b) Where the devolution of the property of the lunatic would be subject to customary law and would not pass under any enactment for the time being in force relation to the administration of property, any person who would have a *spes successionis* according to customary law shall have the same right as a person who would have a spes *successionis* under paragraph (a) of this subsection.

(6) Subject to making due provision for the maintenance of the lunatic in accordance with his station in life, whether out of the capital or income of the property settled or other property or party in one way and partly in another, and to providing, by means of a power of appointment or revocation, or otherwise, for the possibility of the lunatic recovering full capacity, the court may, in making and order under this section, have regard to -

(a) the manner in which the property has been settled or deal with on former occasions.

(b) In the case of land or houses built thereon the claims of relatives, employees or dependants to the use or occupation thereof, and the expediency of settling personal estate to devolve therewith;

(c) the maintenance or education of any illegitimate children of the lunatic and the maintenance of their mother or mothers;

(d) the maintenance of any wife married according to customary law who would not have a *spes successionis* under the preceding subsection, or the maintenance of the parents or natural parents or the lunatic;

(e) the continuation or provision of any pensions and the application of any part of the income for charitable purposes;

(f) the provisions of any testamentary disposition of the lunatic;

(g) the expediency of providing or -

(i) annual or capital charges and powers to create the same;

(ii) discretionary trusts, trusts for effecting or maintaining policies of insurance, powers of appointment, sinking funds for making good loss by fire (in lieu of, or in addition to, insurance) or for any other purpose;

(iii) the extension of any statutory powers of investment, management or otherwise;

(iv) the manner in which any costs are to be raised and, whether out of the settled property or otherwise;

(v) any other matter or thing which, having regard to the nature of the settlement, or the property to be settled, and the management, development, and enjoyment thereof, and to the person who are to take, either successively or otherwise, the court may consider material.

(7) In this section "testamentary disposition" means an instrument executed by the lunatic while of full testamentary capacity, which, if unrevoked, might, on his death, be proved as a will or codicil; and the court may act on such evidence as to the existence or absence of a testamentary disposition as it thinks fit.

(8) At any time before the death of the lunatic the court may, as respects any property remaining subject to the trusts of a settlement made under this section, on being satisfied that any material fact was not disclosed to the court when the settlement was made, or on

account of any substantial change in circumstances, by order vary the settlement in such manner as it thinks fit, and give any consequential directions.

(9) The Chief Judge may make rules for giving effect to the provisions of this section and in particular for compelling information to be furnished respecting, and production of, testamentary dispositions, and the judgement thereof in court, or respecting any person who might receive a benefit under a settlement directed by the court under this section, or for prescribing what notices, if any, of the proceedings are to be served, for desponding with such notices, and, when necessary, for making representation orders.

11. The court may remove a private trustee if the court is satisfied that the continuance of the existing trustee in office may be detrimental to the execution of the trust notwithstanding that misconduct or maladministration has not been proved against him.

12. (1) If, in pursuance of any regulation under this Law, the Public Trustee is authorised to accept by that name probates of will or letters of administration, the court may grant probate Public of a will or letters of administration to the Public Trustee by that name.

(2) For such purpose the court shall consider the Public Trustee as in law entitle equally with any other person or class of person to obtain the grant of letters of administration, save that the consent or citation of the public Trustee shall not be required for the grant of letters of administration to any other person, and that, as between the Public Trustee and the widower, widow or next-of-kin of the deceased, the widower, widow or next-of-kin shall be preferred, unless for good cause shown to the contrary.

13. (1) Any executor who has obtained probate or any administrator who has obtained letters of administration and notwithstanding that he has acted in the administration of the deceased's estate, may, with the sanction of the court, and after such notice to the persons beneficially interested as the court directs, transfer such estate to the Public Trustee for administration either solely or jointly with the continuing executors or administrator, if any.

(2) The order of the court sanctioning such transfer shall, subject to his Law, give to the Public Trustee all the powers of such executor and administrator.

(3) Such executor and administrator shall not be in any way liable in respect of any act or default in reference to such estate subsequent to the date of such order, other than the act or default of himself or of persons other than himself for whose conduct he is in law responsible.

14. The court may, on the application of any person beneficially interested, appoint the Public Trustee, if sufficient cause is shown, in place of all or any existing executors or administrators or of any guardian of infants, or committee or receiver of a person incapable of managing his own affairs.

15. The order of the court granting probate or letters of administration to the Public Trustee, sanctioning the transfer to the Public Trustee, or appointment of the Public Trustee as executor or administrator, of as estate shall, subject to this Law, give to the Public Trustee all the power of the Administrator-General under the Administrator-General Law:

Provided that where at the time of the transfer to, or appointment of the Public Trustee, the estate is fully administered and only the residue is transferred, the Public Trustee shall not be entitle to the remuneration allowed to the Administrator-General when administering estates.

16. In any case where the Public Trustee may be appointed by the court under section 6 (1) or section 8 (1) of this Law, when the persons beneficially interested are minors, or otherwise incapacitated from managing their own affairs, the Public Trustee may himself apply to the appointed.

Liability and Fees

17. The revenues of the Lagos State shall be liable to make good all sums required to discharge any liability which the Public Trustee, if he were a private trustee, would be personally liable to discharge, except where the liability is one to which neither the Public Trustee nor any of his officers has in any way contributed, and which neither he nor any of his officers could by the exercise of reasonable diligence have averted, and in that case the Public Trustee shall not, nor shall the revenues of the Lagos State be subject to any liability.

18. In all cases where the revenues of the Lagos State have to be utilised under the provisions of section 17 hereof, it shall be lawful for the court if it appears that the person holding the office of Public Trustee has acted honestly and ought fairly to be excused for the breach of trust or other act or omission by which the liability was incurred and fro omitting to obtain the directions of the court in the manner in which such liability was incurred to relieve such person either wholly or partly from personal liability for the same under this Law.

19. (1) There shall be charged in respect or the duties of the Public Trustee such fees whether by whether by way of percentage or otherwise, as the state Commissioner may fix.

(2) Any expenses which might be retained or paid out of the trust property, if the Public Trustee was private trustee, shall be so retained or paid, and the fees shall be retained or paid in the like manner as and in addition to such expenses.

(3) Such fees shall be paid into the Treasury.

(4) The incidence of the fees and expenses under this section as between capital and income shall be determined by the Public Trustee.

Supplemental Provisions

20. A person aggrieved by any act or omission or decision of the Public Trustee in relation to any trust may apply to the court, and the court may make such order in the matter as the court thinks just.

21. (1) The Public Trustee shall not, nor shall any of his officers, act under this Law for reward, except as provided by this Law.

(2) The Public Trustee may subject to the regulations made under this Law, employ for the purpose of any trust such legal practitioners, bankers, accountants and brokers, or other person as he considers necessary.

(3) In determining the persons to be so employed in relation to any trust the Public Trustee shall have regard to the interests of the trust, but subjected to this shall, whenever practicable, take into consideration the wishes of the creator of the trust and of the other trustee, if any, and of the beneficiaries, either expressed or as implied by the practice of the creator of the trust, or in the previous management of the trust.

(4) On behalf of the Public Trustee such person as is prescribed may take any oath, make any declaration, verifying any account, give personal attendance at any court or place, and do any act or thing whatsoever which the Public Trustee is required or authorised to take, make verify, give or do.

(5) Where any bond or security would be required from a private person upon the grant to him of administration, or upon his appointment to act in any capacity the Public Trustee, if administration is granted to him or if he is appointed to act in such capacity as aforesaid, shall not be required to give such bond or security, but shall be subject to the same liabilities and duties as if he had given such bond or security.

(6) The entry of the Public Trustee by that name in the books of a company shall not constitute notice of a trust, and a company shall not be entitled to object to enter the name of the Public Trustee is a corporation and, in dealings with property, the fact that the person or one of the persons dealt with is the Public Trustee, shall not of itself constitute notice of a trust.

Investigation and Audit of Trust Accounts

22. (1) Subject to regulations under this Law ad unless the court otherwise orders, the condition and accounts of any trust shall, on an application being made and notice thereof given in the prescribed manner by any trustee or beneficiary, be investigated and audited by such legal practitioner or public accountant as may be agreed on by the applicant and the trustees or, in default of agreement by the Public Trustee or some person appointed by him.

(2) Except with the leave of the court such an investigation or audit shall not be required within twelve months after any such previous investigation or audit and a trustee or beneficiary shall not be appointed under this section to make an investigation or audit.

(3) The person making the investigation or audit, hereinafter called the auditor, shall have a right of access to the books, accounts, and vouchers of the trustee, and to any securities and documents of title held by them on account of the trust, and may require from them such information and explanation as are necessary for the performance of his duties.

(4) Upon the completion of the investigation and audit the auditor shall forward to the applicant and to every trustee a copy of the accounts, together with a report thereon, and a certificate signed by him to the effect that the accounts exhibit a true view of the state of the affairs of the trust and that he has had the securities of the trust fund investments produced to and verified by him or, as the case may be, that such accounts are deficient in such respect as are specified in such certificate.

(5) Every beneficiary under the trust shall, subject to regulations under this Law, be entitled at all reasonable times to inspect and take copies of the accounts, report and certificate, and, at his own expense, to be furnished with copies thereof or extract therefrom.

(6) The auditor may be removed by order of the court, and if any auditor is removed, or resigns, or dies, or becomes incapable of acting before the investigation and audit is completed, a new auditor may be appointed in his place in like manner as the original auditor.

(7) The remuneration of the auditor and the other expenses of the investigation and audit shall be such as may be prescribed, and shall, unless the Public Trustee otherwise directs, be borne by the estate.

(8) In the event of the Public Trustee so directing, he may order such expenses to be borne by the applicant or by the trustee personally or partly by them and partly by the applicant.

(9) If the person having custody of any documents to which the auditor has a right of access under this section fails or refuses to allow him to have access thereof or in any wise obstructs the investigation or audit, the auditor may apply to the court, and thereupon the court shall make such order as it thinks just.

(10) Any person who in any statement of accounts, report or certificate required for the purpose of this section willfully makes a statement false in any material particular shall be liable on summary conviction to imprisonment for twelve months or to a fine of two hundred naira, or to both.

Regulations

23. The Executive Council may make regulations for carrying into effect the objects of this Law and in particular for all or any of the following purpose -

(a) prescribing the trusts or duties which the Public Trustee is authourised to accept or undertake, and the security, if any, to be given by the Public Trustee and his officers;

(b) the transfer to and from the Public Trustee of any property;

(c) the accounts to be kept and the audit thereof;

(d) the establishment and regulation of any branch office; (e) excluding any trust from the operation of this law or any part thereof.

24. This Law shall not have effect -

(a) in relation to any matter in respect of which the Federal Public Trustee shall have commenced to function at the date of the commencement of this Law and in respect of which he is willing to continue to function; nor.

(b) in relation to any matter which it is agree between the Federal Public Trustee and the Public Trustee appointed under this Law can more conveniently be dealt with by the Federal Trustee.

CHAPTER 3 - Unit Trust

575. In this Chapter of this Part -

"auditor" means a member of a body of accountants from time to time recognized by an Act or Decree for the purpose of this Chapter of this Part and appointed as auditor of the trust by managers with the approval of the trustees; "authorised unit trust scheme" means any unit scheme that is authorised by the Commission and registered in the register maintained by the Commission for the purpose of this Chapter of this Part;

"dealing in securities" means doing any of the following things (whether as a principal or as an agent), that is to say, making or offering to make with any person to enter into inducing or attempting to induce any person to enter into or offer to enter into any agreement for or with a view to acquiring, holding or disposing of securities or any other property, or any agreement the purpose or pretended purpose of which is to secure a profit to any of the parties from the yield of securities or by reference to fluctuations in the value of securities;

"filing" means delivery to the Commission throu7gh mails or otherwise of all papers or application required to be filled with the Commission pursuant to this Part and regulations made under it; and the date on which the papers or applications are actually received by the Commission at its principal office shall be the date of filing them;

"holder" means any investors or beneficiary who has acquired units or the unit trust scheme and trust deed, and is entitled to a pro rata share of dividends, interest or other income of the securities comprised in the unit;

"issuer" means the person performing the duties of a manager pursuant to the provisions of the trust under which the units are issued;

"manager" under a unit trust scheme, means the person in whom are vested the powers of management relating to property for the time being subject to any trust created in pursuance of the scheme;

"prospectus" includes offer for sale, advertisement, circular, letter, notice, scheme of arrangement, or other equivalent document published or circulated or proposed to be published or circulated relating to the unit trust scheme; "register" means the register established and maintained for the purposes of this Chapter of this Part;

"trust deed" means the agreement drawn up between the trustees and the manager for regulating the operation of a unit trust scheme;

"trustee" under a unit trust scheme means the person in whom the property for the time being subject to any trust created in pursuance of the scheme is or may be vested in accordance with the terms of the trust;

"units" in relation to a unit trust scheme, means any units (described whether as units or otherwise) into which are divided the beneficial interest in the assets subject to any trust created under the scheme:

"unit trust scheme" means any arrangement made for the purpose, or having the effect, of providing facilities for the participation of the public as beneficiaries under a trust in profits or income arising from acquisition holding, management or disposal of securities of any other property whatsoever.

576. (1) Notwithstanding anything contained in this Act, no person shall establish or operate a unit trust scheme or carry on or purport to carry on the business of dealing in units or otherwise) unless such scheme is authorised by any and registered with the Commission.

(2) An application for authorization under this section shall be in the form prescribed by the Commission and shall be accompanied by such documents as may be specified, from time to time, by the Commission.

(3) upon application to the Commission in accordance with this Act by the manager under a unit trust scheme, the Commission may authorised and register it but only if -

(a) the Commission is satisfied that the competence in respect of matters of the kind with which they would be concerned in relation to a unit trust scheme and probity of the manager and trustee are such as to render them suitable to act as manager and trustee, respectively, under the scheme;

(b) the manager under the scheme is a body corporate that is incorporated under this Act and having a minimum paid-up capital W250,000;

(c) the trustee under the scheme is a body corporate such as a bank or an insurance company licensed under the relevant statute and having a minimum paid up capital of N600,000;

(d) the Commission is satisfied that the scheme is such that the effective control over the affairs of the company which is the manager under the scheme is and shall be exercised independently of the company which is the trustee under the scheme;

(e) the Commission is satisfied that the trust deed is incompliance with the provisions of this Act and the rules and regulations for the time being in force thereunder; and a copy of the trust deed aforesaid deposited with the Commission; and

(f) the name of the scheme is not, in the opinion of the Commission, undesirable.

(4) The Commission may refuse to authorise a unit trust scheme if it fails to comply with the provisions of this Chapter and shall so notify the manager and the trustee under the scheme stating its reasons for refusal within thirty days of such refusal.

(5) Upon authorisation of a unit trust scheme, the Commission shall certify that the scheme is so authorised.

PART -XI COLLECTIVE INVESTMENT SCHEMES

123. (1) In this Decree and subject to this section, a "Collective Investment Scheme" means -

(a) any arrangement with respect to property of any description, including money, the purpose or effect of which is to enable persons taking part in the arrangements (whether by becoming owners of the property or any part of it or otherwise) to participate in or receive profits or income arising from the acquisition, holding, management or disposal of the property or sums paid out of such profits or income;

(b) any arrangement described in paragraph (a) of this subsection in which the participants do not have day to day control over the management of the property underlying the arrangement notwithstanding that they have a right to be consulted or to give directives;

(c) any arrangement as set out in paragraph (a)or (b) of this subsection in which participants pool their contributions for the purpose of sharing the profits or income arising from the management of their money or property solely from the efforts of a third party

(2) where any arrangement provide for such pooling as is mentioned in paragraph (c) of subsection (1) of this section in relation to separate parts of the property, the arrangement shall not be regarded as constituting a single collective investment scheme unless the participants are entitled to exchange rights in one part for rights in another.

(3) The following are not collective investment schemes:

(a) arrangements operated by a person otherwise than by way of business;

(b) arrangements where each of the participants carries on a business other than investment business enters into the arrangements for commercial purpose related to that business;

(c) arrangements where each of the participants is a body corporate in the same group as the operator;

124. In this Part -

"auditor" means a member of a body of accountants, from time to time, recognized by an Act or Decree or any other enactment and appointed as auditor of the trust by managers with the approval of the trustees;

"authorised unit trust scheme" means any unit trust scheme which is authorized by the Commission and registered in the register maintained by the Commission for the purpose of this Part;

"dealing in securities" means doing any of the following things (whether as a principal or as an agent), that is, making or offering to make with any person, or inducing or attempting to induce any person to enter into or *offer* to enter into any agreement for or with a view to acquiring, holding or disposing of securities or any other property, or any agreement the purpose or pretended purpose of which is to secure a profit to any of the parties from the yield of securities or by reference to fluctuations in the value of securities;

"filing" means delivery to the Commission through mails or otherwise of all papers or applications required to be filed with the Commission pursuant to this Decree and regulations made thereunder, and the date on which the papers or applications are actually received by the Commission at its principal office shall be the date of filing the papers or applications;

"holder" means any investor or beneficiary who has acquired units of the unit trust scheme and trust deed, and is entitled to a prorata share of dividends, interest or other income of the securities comprised in the unit;

"issuer" means the person performing the duties of a manager pursuant to the provisions of the trust under which the units are issued;

"manager" under a unit trust scheme means the person in whom are vested the powers of management relating to;

property for the time being subject to any trust created in pursuance of the scheme;

"prospectus" includes offer for sale, advertisement, circular, letter, notice, scheme of arrangement, or other equivalent document published or circulated relating to the unit trust scheme;

"register" means the register established and maintained for the purposes of this Part;

"trust deed" means the agreement drawn up between the trustees and the manager for regulating the operation of a unit trust scheme;

"trustee" under a unit trust scheme means the person in whom the property for the time being subject to any trust created in pursuance of the scheme is or may be vested in accordance with the terms of the trust;

"units" in relation to a unit trust scheme, means any unit (described whether as unit or otherwise into which are divided the beneficial interest in the assets subject to any trust created under the scheme:

"unit trust scheme" or "mutual fund" means any agreement made for the purpose, or having the effect, of providing facilities for the participation of the public as beneficiaries under a trust in profits or income arising from acquisition, holding, management or disposal of securities or any other property whatsoever.

125. (1) Notwithstanding anything contained in this Decree, no person shall establish or operate a unit trust scheme or carry on or purport to carry on the business of dealing in units of a trust scheme (described whether as units or otherwise) unless such scheme is authorised by and registered with the Commission.

(2) An application for authorisation under this section shall be in the form prescribed by the Commission and shall be accompanied by such documents as may be specified, from time to time, by the Commission.

(3) Upon application to the commission in accordance with this Decree by the manager under a unit trust scheme, the Commission may authorise and register if but only if:

(a) the Commission is satisfied that the competence in respect of matter of the kind with which they would be concerned in relation to a unit trust scheme and probity of the manager and trustee are such as to render them suitable to act as manager and trustee respectively under the scheme;

(b) the manager under the scheme is a body corporate which is incorporated under the Companies and Allied Matters Decree 1990 and having a minimum paid-up capital of N20,000,000;

(c) the trustee under the scheme is a body corporate such as a bank or an insurance company licensed under the Insurance Decree 1997 having a minimum paid up capital of N40,000,000;

(d) the Commission is satisfied that the scheme is such that the effective control of affairs of the scheme is vested in the manager and is exercised independently of the company which is the trustee under the scheme;

(e) the Commission is satisfied that the trust deed is in compliance with the provisions of this Decree and the rules and regulations for the time being in force thereunder; and a copy of the trust deed aforesaid is deposited with the Commission; and

(f) the name of the scheme is not, in the opinion of the Commission, undesirable.

(4) The Commission may refuse to authorise a unit trust scheme if it fails to comply with the provisions of this Part of this Decree and shall so notify the manager and the trustee under the scheme stating its

reasons for refusal within thirty days of such refusal.

(5) Upon authorisation of a unit trust scheme, the Commission shall certify that the scheme is so authorised.

126. (1) It shall not be lawful for any person, directly or indirectly to deal in units of a trust scheme (described whether as units or otherwise) unless such units have been duly registered with the Commission.

(2) A unit may be registered pursuant to this Decree by the issuer filing an application with the Commission in accordance with the provisions of this Part of this Decree and the rules and regulations thereunder.

(3) Any application for registration of units filed pursuant to this section shall become effective on the sixtieth day after filing thereof or such earlier date as the Commission may determine having due regard to the adequacy of the information contained in such application and registration shall be deemed affective only as to the units specified therein as proposed to be offered.

(4) The Commission shall establish and maintain a register of units and unit trust schemes (in this Part of this Decree referred to as the "register").

127. (1) It shall not be lawful for any manager or trustee under a unit trust scheme to make any alteration in the deed in which are expressed the trusts of an authorised scheme or to make any change in the name of an authorised scheme without prior approval of the Commission.

(2) Where the manager or trustee under a unit trust scheme fails to comply with subsection (1) of this section, he commits an offence and is liable on conviction to a fine of 450, 000 and in addition to a penalty of N5,000 per day for the period during which the default subsists.

128. (1) Subject to the provisions of this section, the Commission may revoke the authorization of a scheme if -

    (a)   there is a contravention of any provision of this Part of the Decree or of any rule or regulation made thereunder; or

    (b)   there is a contravention of any of the conditions specified in subsection (3) (b), (c) and (e) of section 125 of this Part of this Decree; or

    (c)   the Commission is no longer satisfied in respect of the matter specified in subsection (3) (a), (d) and (f) of section 125 of this Part of this Decree; or

    (d)   the interest of the holders of units created under the scheme so requires.

  (2) The Commission shall before such revocation -

    (a)   notify the manager and the trustee under the scheme and the manager and trustee may within twenty-one days from the date of such notification make representations in writing to the Commission in respect of the proposed revocation;

(b) consider any representation duly made by the manager and trustee under the scheme.

(3) The Commission shall communicate its decision to revoke its authorisation of the unit trust scheme within thirty days after the making of the representations or if none are made within thirty days after the last day for making of the representations under this section.

129. (1) Any letter, notice, circular or document prepared by the manager for the purpose of offering units of a unit trust scheme to the public shall be approved by the trustee and submitted to the Commission for approval before such letter, notice, circular or document is published.

(2) There shall be included in a document of the kind referred to in subsection (1) of this section, information in relation to such matters (if any) as may be specified, from time to time, by the Commission.

130. (1) Any manager under a unit trust scheme who offers or sells by means of a letter, notice, circular, document or oral communication which includes an untrue statement of a material fact or omits to state a material fact necessary in order to make the statements, in the light of the circumstances under which they were made, not misleading (the purchaser not knowing of such untruth or omission and who shall not sustain the burden of proof that he did not known, and in the exercise of reasonable care could not have know, of such untruth or omission), is liable to the person purchasing such units who may bring an action before the Investments and Securities Tribunal established under this Decree (in this Decree referred to as "the Tribunal") to recover the consideration paid for such units, or for damages if he no longer owns the units.

(2) No action shall be maintained to enforce any liability under subsection (1) of this section, unless brought within two years after discovery of the untrue statement or after such discovery ought to have been made by the exercise of reasonable care.

131. (1) Whenever the holder of units of an authorised unit trust scheme so requests, the manager under the scheme, shall, within the time specified by the Commission, buy from the holder such number of those units as the holder may specify at the price for the time being at which the manager buys units of the scheme.

(2) Whenever the authorisation of a unit trust scheme under this Decree stands revoked, the unit trust scheme shall buy all the units under the manager under scheme at the price for the time being at which the manager buys units of the scheme.

132. (1) No company that is a manager under a nit trust scheme or is a subsidiary or holding company of the manager or a director or a person engaged in the management of such a company shall carry out transactions for itself or himself, or make a profit for itself or himself, from a transaction in any assets held under the scheme.

(2) A company that is a manager under a unit trust scheme or is a subsidiary or holding company of the manager shall not -

    (a) borrow money on behalf of the scheme for the purpose of acquiring securities or other property for the scheme;

    (b) lend money that is subject to the trusts of the scheme to a person to enable him to purchase units of the scheme; or

    (c) mortgage or charge or impose any other encumbrance on any securities or other property subject to the trust of the scheme; or

    (d) engage in any transactions that are not in the interest of unit holders and of the scheme

(3) Any person who contravenes the provisions of this section commits an offence and is liable on conviction to a fine of not less than equal the amount of profits made from any such transaction or to a fine of N20, 000 whichever is higher.

133. Any provision in the trust deed in which are expressed the trusts created in pursuance of an authorised unit trust scheme shall be void in so far as it would have the effect of exempting the trustee under the scheme from or indemnifying it against liability for breach of trust where, having regard to the provisions of the trust deed conferring on him any powers, authorities or discretion, he fails to exercise the degree of care and diligence required of him as trustee.

134. (1) The manager of an authorised unit trust scheme shall cause proper books of account to be kept and annual accounts to be prepared which shall give a fair and true view of the affairs of the scheme during each year covered by the accounts and the accounts shall be audited by a person appointed as auditor by the manager under the scheme with the consent of the trustee under the scheme.

(2) A copy of the auditor's report on the accounts and of such account certified, by an auditor shall be sent by the manager to the Commission and also published in national newspapers within three months after the end of the period to which the accounts relate or as the Commission may, from time to time, specify.

(3) The auditor shall certify that the unit trust scheme has been operated within the provisions of this Decree and the regulations prescribed by the Commission.

(4) The manager under the scheme shall call an annual general meeting of unit holders with the consent of the trustee not latter than four months after each year to consider the accounts and other matters affecting the scheme.

(5) An extraordinary general meeting of the unit holder may be convened

    (a) by the manager with the consent of the trustee; or

    (b) at the request of the trustees; or

    (c) by the requisition of twenty-five percent of the unit holders; or

    (d) by the court on application by a member where the court is satisfied that it is just and equitable so to do.

135. The calculation of prices at which units of any unit trust scheme may be bought or sold shall be done in accordance with the formula laid down by the Commission in the rules and regulations made under this Decree.

136. Every manager of an authorised unit trust scheme shall invest only in

(a) securities specified under the Trustee Investment Act as amended from time to time; and

(b) such other investments as the Commission may, from time to time; approve.

137. (1) The Commission shall have the power at any time to inspect documents in respect of any unit trust scheme

(2) The Commission may investigate and report on the administration of any unit trust scheme, if it appears to it that it is in the interest of holders of units under the scheme to do so or the matter is in the public interest

(3) If an officer or agent of the manager or trustee whose affairs are being investigated or inspected by virtue of this section refuses to produce to the Commission any document which it is his duty under this section so to produce or refuses to answer any question which is put to him by the Commission with respect to the unit trust scheme, he commits an offence and is liable on conviction to a fine of not less than N20,000.

138. (1) The Commission may make regulation as to the constitution and management of authorised unit trust schemes, the powers and duties of the manager and trustee of any such scheme and the rights and obligations if persons participating in any such scheme.

(2) Without prejudice to the generality of subsection (1) If this section, the Commission may make regulations finder this section -

(a) as to the issue and redemption of the units under the scheme;

(b) as to the expenses of the scheme and the means of meeting them;

(c) for the appointment, removal, powers and duties of an auditor for the scheme; borrowing powers exercisable in relation to the scheme;

(e) requiring the keeping of records with respect to the transactions and financial position of the scheme and for the inspection of those records;

(f) requiring the preparation of periodic reports with respect to the scheme and the furnishing of those reports to the participants and the Commission; and

(g) with respect to the amendment of the scheme.

(3) Regulations made under this section -

(a) may make provision as to the contents of the trust deed, including provision requiring any of the matters mentioned in subsection (2) of this section to be dealt within the trust deed;

(b) shall be binding on the manager, trustee and participants independently of the contents of the trust deed and, in the case of the participants, shall have effect as if contained in it;

(c) shall not impose limits on the remuneration payable to the manager of a scheme;

(d) may contain such incidental and transitional provisions as the Commission thinks necessary or expedient.

139. (1) The manager of an authorised unit trust scheme shall give written notice to the Commission of -

(a) any proposed alteration to the scheme; and

(b) any proposal to replace the unit trustee of the scheme.

(2) Any notice given in respect of a proposed alteration involving a change in the trust deed shall be accompanied by a certificate signed by a solicitor to the effect that the change will not affect the compliance of the trust deed with the regulations made under section 138 of this Decree

(3) The trustee of an authorised unit trust scheme shall give written notice to the Commission of any proposal to replace the manager of the scheme.

(4) Effect shall not be given to any such proposal unless - (a) the Commission has given its approval to the proposal; or one month has elapsed since the date on which the notice was given under subsection (1) or (2) of this section without the Commission having notified the manager or trustee that the proposal is not approved.

(5) Neither the manager nor the trustee of an authorised unit trust scheme shall be replaced except by persons who satisfy the requirements of section 140 of this Decree or regulations made thereunder.

140. (1) The manager of an authorised unit trust scheme shall not engage in any activities other than those mentioned in subsection (2) of this section.

(2) The activities referred to in subsection (1) of this section are -

(a) acting as manager of -

(i) a unit trust scheme,

(ii) an open-ended investment company or any other body corporate whose business consists of investing its funds with the aim of spreading investment risk and giving its members the benefit of the expert management of its funds by or on behalf of that body, or

(iii) any other collective investment scheme under which the contributions of the participants and the profits or income out of which payments are to be made to them are pooled;

(b) activities for the purpose of or in connection with those activities mentioned in paragraph (a) of this subsection.

141. (1) The Commission may make regulations requiring the manager of an authorised unit trust scheme to submit to him and publish or make particulars available to the public on request of a document ("scheme particulars") containing information about the scheme and complying with such requirements as are specified in the regulations

(2) Regulations under this section may require the manager of an authorised unit trust scheme to submit and publish or make available revised or further scheme particulars if -

(a) there is a significant change affecting any matter contained in such particulars previously published or made available whose inclusion was required by the regulations; or

(b) a significant new matter arises where the inclosing of information in respect of which would have been required in previous particulars if it had arisen when those particulars were prepared.

(3) Regulations under this section may provide for the payment by the person or persons who in accordance with the regulations are treated as responsible for any scheme particulars of compensation to any person who has become or agreed to become a participant in the scheme and suffered loss as a result of any untrue or misleading statement in the particulars or the omission from them of any matter required by the regulations to be included.

(4) Regulations under this section shall not affect any liability which any person may incur apart from the regulations.

142. (1) If it appears to the Commission -

(a) that any of the requirements for the making of an order declaring a scheme to be an authorised unit trust scheme are no longer satisfied;

(b) that the exercise of the power conferred by this subsection is desirable in the interests of participants or potential participants in the scheme; or

(c) without prejudice to paragraph (b) of this subsection, that the manager or trustee of such a scheme has contravened any provision of this Decree or any rules or regulations made thereunder or, in purported compliance with any such provisions has furnished the Commission with false, inaccurate or misleading information or has contravened any prohibition or requirement imposed under this Decree,

the Commission may give a directive -

(a) requiring the manager of the scheme to cease the issue or redemption, or both the issue and redemption of units under the scheme on a date specified in the directive until such further date as is specified in that order or directive; or

(b) requiring the manager and trustee of the scheme to wind it up by such date as is specified in the directive or if no date is specified, as soon as practicable.

(2) The revocation of the order declaring an authorised unit trust scheme to be such a scheme shall not affect the operation of any directive under subsection (1) of this

section which is then in force; and a directive may be given under that subsection in relation to a scheme in the case of which the order declaring it to be an authorised unit trust scheme has been revoked if a directive under that subsection was already in force at the time of revocation.

143. (1) Where the Commission proposes to -

    (a) refuse an application for an order under section 142 of this Decree; or

    (b) revoke such an order otherwise than at the request of the manager or trustee of the scheme;

        (i) it shall give the applicants or, as the case may be, the manager and trustee of the scheme written notice of its intention to do so stating the reasons for which it proposes to act and giving particulars of the rights conferred by subsection (2) of this section.

(2) A person on whom a notice is served under subsection (1) of this section may, within twenty-one days of the date of service, make written representations to the Commission and, if desired, oral representations to a person appointed for that purpose by the Commission.

(3) The Commission shall have regard to any representations made in accordance with subsection (2) of this section in determining whether to refuse the application or revoke the order, as the case may be.

144. (1) In any case in which the Commission has power to give a direction under subsection (1) of section 139 of this Decree in relation to an authorised unit trust scheme or, by virtue of subsection (2) of that section in relation to a scheme which has much a scheme it may to the Tribunal.

    (a) for an order removing the manager of trustee of both the manager and the trustee of the scheme and replacing either or both of them with a person or persons nominated by it and appearing to it to satisfy the requirements of section 140 of this Decree; or

    (b) if it appears to the Commission that no suitable person satisfying those requirements is available, for an order removing the manager or trustee, or both the manager and trustee, and appointing an authorised person to wind the scheme up.

(2) On an application under this section to the Tribunal it may make such order as it thinks fit; on the application of the Commission, rescind any such order as is mentioned in subsection (1)(b) of this section and substitute such an order as is mentioned in subsection (1)(a) of this section.

(3) The Commission shall give written notice of the making of an application under this section to the manager and trustee of the scheme concerned and take such steps as it considers appropriate for bringing the making of the application to the attention of the participants.

Supplemental

145. (1) The Commission may appoint one or more competent inspectors to investigate and report on -

(a) the affairs of, or of the manager or trustee of any authorised unit trust scheme;

(b) the affairs of, or of the operator or trustee of any recognised scheme so far as relating to activities carried on in the Federal Republic of Nigeria; or

(c) the affairs of, or of the operator or trustee of, any other collective investment scheme if it appears to the Commission that it is in the interest of the participants to do so or that the matter is of public concern.

(2) Any inspector appointed under subsection (1) of this section to investigate the affairs of, or of the manager, trustee or operator of any scheme may also if he thinks it necessary for the purposes of that investigation, investigate the affairs of or the manager, trustee or operator of, any other such scheme as is mentioned in that subsection whose manager, trustee or operator is the same person as the manager, trustee or operator of the first mentioned scheme.

(3) Any person shall not under this section be required to disclose any information or produce any document which he would be entitled to refuse to disclose or produce on grounds of legal professional privilege in judicial proceedings or on grounds of confidentiality as between a client and professional legal adviser in proceedings in any court except that a lawyer may be required to furnish the name and address of his client.

(4) Where a person claims a lien on a document its production under this section shall be without prejudice to the lien.

(5) Nothing in this section shall require a person carrying on the business of banking to disclose any information or produce any document relating to the affairs of a customer unless -

(a) the customer is a person who the inspector has reason to believe may be able to give information relevant to the investigation; and (b) the   Commission   is satisfied that the disclosure or production is necessary for the purposes of the investigation.

(6) An inspector appointed under this section of this Decree may, and if so directed by the Commission, make interim reports to the Commission and on the conclusion of his investigation shall make a final report to the Commission.

(7) A report made under subsection (8) of this section shall be written or printed as the Commission may direct and the Commission may, if it thinks fit -

(a) furnish a copy, on request and on payment of the prescribed fee, to the manager, trustee or operator or any participant in a scheme under investigation or any other person whose conduct is referred to in the report; and

(b) cause the report to be published.

146. (1) As from the commencement of this Decree the Commission shall register collective investment schemes falling within the category of community savings schemes which includes "Esusu" schemes and such other similar schemes operating within Nigeria.

(2) The registration of the community savings schemes referred to in subsection (1) of this section shall be for statistical purposes only and such schemes shall not be subject to the other provisions of this Part of this Decree regulating the activities and operations of other collective investment schemes registered under this Part of this Decree.

(3) The Commission shall prescribe forms for the registration of the schemes referred to in subsection (1) of this section.

(4) The Commission shall not charge any registration fee for services rendered under this section of this Decree.

147. (1) It shall be lawful for a body corporate incorporated for the sole purpose of acquiring intermediate or long term interests in real estate or property development to raise funds from the capital market through the issuance of securities which shall have the following characteristics -

  (a) an income certificate giving the investor a right to a share of the income of any property or property development; and

  (b) an ordinary share in the body corporate giving the investor voting rights in the management of that body corporate.

(2) It shall be lawful under this Decree for a trust to be constituted for the sole purpose of acquiring a property on a "trust for sale" for the investors.

(3) The trust referred to in subsection (2) of this section shall have the following characteristics.

  (a) the investors shall acquire units in the trust through which they shall be entitled to receive periodic distribution of income and participate in any capital appreciation of the property concerned; and

  (b) the investors shall also be entitled to retain control over their investments by investing directly in a particular property rather than in a portfolio of investments.

(4) The Commission shall, from time to time, make rules and regulations regulating the activities of the asset backed securities of the corporate body and trust referred to in subsections (1) and (2) of the section.

PART XII - INVESTORS PROTECTION FUND

(c) (1) A Securities Exchange or Capital Trade Point shall establish and maintain a fund to be known as the Investors Protection Fund which shall be administered by its governing board (hereafter referred to as "the Board") on its behalf.

(2) The assets of the Investors Protection Fund shall be the property of the Securities Exchange or Capital Trade Point but shall be kept separate from all other property and shall be held in trust for the purpose set out in this Part of this Decree.

149. The Investors Protection Fund shall consist of - Public Trustee Law, Laws of Lagos State:

    (a) all moneys paid to the Securities Exchange or Capital Trade Point by member companies in accordance with the provisions of this Part of this Decree;

    (b) the interest and profits, from time to time, accruing from the investment of the Investors Protection Fund;

    (c) all moneys paid to the Investors Protection Fund by a Securities Exchange or Capital Trade Point;

    (d) all moneys recovered by or on behalf of the Securities Exchange or Capital Trade Point in the exercise of any right of action conferred by this Part of this Decree;

    (e) all moneys paid by an insurer pursuant to a contract of insurance or indemnity entered into by the Board; and

    (f) all other moneys lawfully paid into the Investor Protection Fund.

150. All moneys forming a part of an Investors Protection Fund shall be paid or transferred into a separate bank account in Nigeria pending the investment or application of such moneys in accordance with the provisions of this Part of this Decree.

151. Subject to the provisions of this Part of this Decree, there shall, from time to time, be paid out of the Investors Protection Fund of a Securities Exchange or Capital Trade Point such amounts as the Board considers appropriate which amount or amounts shall include -

    (a) the amount of all claims, including costs, allowed by the Board or established against the Securities Exchange or Capital Trade Point under this Part of this Decree;

    (b) all legal and other expenses incurred in investigating or defending claims made under this Part of this Decree or incurred in relation to the Investors Protection Fund or in the exercise by the Boards of the rights, powers and authorities vested in it by this Part of this Decree in relation to the Investors Protection Fund;

    (c) all premiums payable in respect of contracts of insurance or indemnity entered into by the Board;

    (d) the expenses incurred or involved in the administration of the Investors Protection Fund including the salaries and wages of persons employed by the Board in relation thereto; and

(e) all other moneys payable out of the Investors Protection Fund in accordance with the provisions of this Decree.

152. (1) A Securities Exchange or Capital Trade Point shall establish and keep proper books of accounts in relation to its Investors Protection Fund and shall not later than 30th April in each year cause the income and expenditure for the year and a balance sheet to be made out as at the preceding 31st December in respect of such accounts.

(2) A Board of a Securities Exchange or Capital Trade Point shall appoint an auditor to audit the accounts of any Investors Protection Fund established by it.

(3) The auditor appointed by the Board shall regularly and fully audit the accounts of the Investors Protection Fund and shall complete the audit not later than 30th May to enable the audited accounts to be submitted by the Board to the Commission not later than 30th June of the calendar year following that in which the accounts relate.

153. (1) The Board may for the purpose of management of the Investors Protection Fund appoint a management sub-committee of not less than 3 and not more than 5 persons.

(2) The Board may by resolution delegate to a subcommittee appointed under subsection (1) this section all or any of its powers.

(3) Any power, authority or discretion so delegated by the Board may be exercised by members forming a majority of the sub-committee as if that power, authority or discretion had been conferred on a majority of the members of the sub-committee.

(4) Any such delegation by the Board may at any time in like manner be rescinded or varied.

(5) The Board may at any time remove any member of a sub-committee appointed by it under this section and may fill any vacancy in the sub-committee howsoever arising.

(6) A decision of a sub-committee of the Board shall be of no effect until it is confirmed or ratified by the Board.

154. The Investors Protection Fund shall consist of such amount as may by regulation be approved by the Commission, from time to time, to be paid to the credit of the Investors Protection Fund on the establishment of a Securities Exchange or Capital Trade Point under this Decree.

155. If for whatever reasons the Investors protection Fund falls below the minimum amount approved for a Securities Exchange or Capital Trade Point the management sub-committee shall take steps to make up the deficiency -

(a) by transferring to the Investors Protection Fund an amount which is equal to the deficiency from other funds of the Securities Exchange or Capital Trade Point; or

(b) in the event that there are insufficient funds to transfer under paragraph (a) of this section, by determining the amount which each member company shall contribute to the Fund.

156. (1) If at any time the amount available in an Investors Protection Fund is not sufficient to satisfy the liabilities which are ascertained against a Securities Exchange or Capital Trade Point, the Board may impose on every member company a levy of such amount as it thinks fit; or if approved by the Commission, shall impose a levy of such sum which shall in the aggregate be the equivalent to the amount specified in the approval.

(2) The amount of such levy shall be paid within the time and in the manner specified by the Board either generally or in relation to any particular case.

157. (1) A Securities Exchange or Capital Trade Point may, from time to time, from its general funds give or advance, on such terms as the Board thinks fit, any sums of money to its Investor Protection Fund.

(2) Any moneys advanced under subsection (1) of this section may, from time to time, be repaid from the Investors Protection Fund to the general funds of the Securities Exchange or Capital trade Point.

158. Any moneys in an Investors Protection Fund which are not immediately required for its purposes may be invested by the Board in any manner in which trustees are for the time being authorised by the Trustee Investment Act to invest trust funds.

159. (1) Subject to this Part of this Decree, an Investors Protection Fund shall be held and applied for the purpose of compensating persons who suffer pecuniary loss from any defalcation committed by a member company or any of its directors or employees in relation to any money or other property which, was entrusted or received by a member company or any of its directors or employees whether before or after the commencement of this Decree in the course of or in connection with the business of that company.

(2) If, after taking into account all ascertained or contingent liabilities of an Investors Protection Fund the Board considers that the assets of the Fund so permit, the Board may decide to increase the total amount which may be applied from an Investors Protection Fund and shall inform the Commission accordingly.

(3) Notwithstanding any provision in subsection (2) of this section the Commission may, by order, direct the Board to increase the total amount which shall be applied from an Investors Protection Fund to a particular member company in payment to persons who suffer loss through defalcations by that particular member company or any of its directors or by any of that member company's employees

(4) For the purposes of this section, "a director of a member company" includes a person who has at the time of the defalcation in question been or has ceased to be a director of a member company if, at the time of the defalcation the person claiming

compensation has reasonable grounds for believing that person to be a director of a member company.

160. (1) Subject to this part of this Decree, every person who suffers Pecuniary loss as provided in section 159 of this Decree shall be entitled to claim compensation from the Investors Protection Fund and to take appropriate judicial proceedings as provided in this Decree against a Securities Exchange or Capital Trade Point to establish the claim.

(2) Subject to subsection (3) of this section, a person shall not have any claim against an Investors Protection Fund in respect of a defalcation concerning money or other property which prior to the commission of the defalcation had in due course of the administration of a trust ceased to be under the control of the director or directors of the member company concerned.

(3) Subject to this Part of this Decree, the amount which any claimant shall be entitled to claim as compensation from an Investors Protection Fund shall be the amount of the actual pecuniary loss suffered by him (including reasonable cost of disbursements incidental to the making and proving of his claim) less the amount or value of all moneys or other benefits received or receivable by him from any source other than the Fund in reduction for the loss.

(4) In addition to any compensation payable under this Part of this Decree, interest shall be payable out of the Investors Protection Fund concerned on the amount of the compensation, less any amount attributable to costs and disbursements, at the rate of 5 *per cent* per annum calculated from the day upon which the defalcation was committed and continuing until the day upon which the claim is satisfied.

161. (1) The Commission may cause to be published in a daily newspaper circulating generally in Nigeria a notice, in or to the effect of the form prescribed, specifying a date, not being earlier than three months after the said publication, on which claims for compensation from the Investors Protection Fund, in relation to the person specified in the notice, may be made.

(2) A claim for compensation from an Investors Protection Fund in respect of a defalcation shall be made in writing to the Board within 6 months after the claimant became aware of the defalcation, and any claim which is not so made shall be barred unless the Commission otherwise determines.

(3) No action for damages shall lie against a Securities Exchange or Capital Trade Point or against any member or employee of a Securities Exchange or Capital Trade Point or of a Board or management sub-committee by reason of any notice published in good faith and without malice for the purposes of this section.

162. The Commission may, subject to this Part of this Decree, allow and settle any claims for compensation from an Investors Protection Fund at any time after the commission of the defalcation in respect of which the claim arose.

163. (1) Where in any proceedings brought to establish a claim the Tribunal is satisfied that the defalcation on which the claim is founded was actually committed and that otherwise the claimant has a valid claim, the Tribunal shall by order.

    (a) declare the fact and the date of the defalcation and the amount of the claim payable; and

    (b) direct that the Investors Protection Fund concerned allows the claim so declared and deal with the same in accordance with the provisions of this Part of this Decree.

(2) The Tribunal may make rules of practice and procedure generally for proceedings under this Part of this Decree.

(3) In any proceedings under this Part of this Decree all questions of costs shall be at the discretion of the Tribunal.

164. The Commission may, from time to time, require any person to produce and deliver any securities, documents or statements of evidence necessary to support any claim made or necessary for the purpose of either of exercising its rights against a member company or the Management of Property - The Trust Option In Nigeria directors thereof or any other person concerned or enabling criminal proceedings to be taken against any person in respect of a defalcation, and in default of delivery such first-mentioned person, the Commission may disallow any claim by him under this Part of this Decree.

165. On payment out of an Investors Protection Fund of any moneys in respect of any claim under this Part of this Decree, the Securities Exchange and Capital Trade Point Public Trustee Law, Laws of Lagos State shall be subrogated to the extent of payment to all the rights and remedies of the claimant in relation to the loss suffered by him from the defalcation.

166. No moneys or other property belonging to a Securities Exchange or Capital Trade Point, other than the Investors Protection Fund, shall be available for the payment of any claim under this Part of this Decree whether the claim is allowed by the Commission or is made the subject of an order of the Tribunal.

167. (1) Where the amount at credit in an Investors Protection Fund is insufficient to pay the whole amount of all claims against it which have been allowed or in respect of which orders have been made, then the amount at the credit in the Investors Protection Fund shall, subject to subsection (2) of this section, be apportioned between the claimants in such manner as the Commission thinks equitable, and any such claim so far as it then remains unpaid shall be charged against future receipts of the Investors Protection Fund and paid out of the Investors Protection Fund when moneys are available therein.

    (2) Upon payment out of the Investors Protection Fund of the total amount, all the other claims against the Investors Protection Fund which may thereafter arise or be made in

respect of defalcations by or in connection with the said member company shall be absolutely discharged.

168. (1) A Securities Exchange or Capital Trade Point may in its discretion enter into any contract with any person carrying on fidelity or investor protection insurance business in Nigeria by which the Securities Exchange or Capital Trade Point shall be indemnified to the extent and in the manner provided by the contract against liability in respect of claims under this Part of this Decree.

(2) A contract may be entered into in relation to member companies generally or in relation to any particular member company or member companies named therein or in relation of members companies with the exclusion of any particular member company or member companies named therein.

(3) No action shall lie against a Securities Exchange or Capital Trade Point or agains any member or employee of a Securities Exchange and Capital Trade Point or against any member of its management for injury alleged to have been suffered by any member company by reason of the publication in good faith of a statement that any contract entered into under this section does or does not apply with respect to it.

169. No claimant against an Investors Protection Fund shall have any rights of action against any person or body of persons with whom a contract of insurance or indemnity is made under this Part of this Decree in respect of such contract, or have any right or claim with respect to any money paid by the insurer in accordance with any such contract.

170. In this Part of this Decree:

"Board" means the management sub-committee, Council or a body responsible for the management of a Securities Exchange or Capital Trade Point;

"Investor Protection Fund" or Fund" means an Investors Protection Fund establishment under this Part;

"Securities Exchange or Capital Trade Point" in relation to an Investors Protection Fund, means the Securities Exchange or Capital Trade Point which established the Fund.

Index

www.ingramcontent.com/pod-product-compliance
Lightning Source LLC
Chambersburg PA
CBHW021604210326
41599CB00010B/597